D1154043

QUEER WARS

PAUL ROBINSON

Queer

The University of Chicago Press

Wars

The New Gay Right and Its Critics

CHICAGO & LONDON

WITHDRAWN

HQ
76.85
,R63
2005
386058

PAUL ROBINSON is the Richard W. Lyman Professor in the
Humanities at Stanford University. He is the author of a
number of books, including *Opera, Sex, and Other Vital
Matters* and *Gay Lives: Homosexual Autobiography from John
Addington Symonds to Paul Monette*, both published by the
University of Chicago Press.

The University of Chicago Press, Chicago 60637
The University of Chicago Press, Ltd., London
© 2005 by The University of Chicago
All rights reserved. Published 2005
Printed in the United States of America

14 13 12 11 10 09 08 07 06 05   1 2 3 4 5

ISBN: 0-226-72200-7 (cloth)

Library of Congress Cataloging-in-Publication Data

Robinson, Paul A., 1940–
  Queer wars : the new gay right and its critics / Paul
Robinson.
    p. cm.
  Includes index.
  ISBN 0-226-72200-7 (cloth : alk. paper)
  1. Gay conservatives.   I. Title.
HQ76.85.R63 2005
306.76'6—dc22   2004005111

♾ The paper used in this publication meets the minimum
requirements of the American National Standard for
Information Sciences—Permanence of Paper for Printed
Library Materials, ANSI Z39.48-1992.

FOR UTE & SUSAN

Contents

Acknowledgments

I want to thank the Andrew W. Mellon Foundation for supporting my fellowship at the Center for Advanced Study in the Behavioral Sciences, where I spent an enjoyable year writing this book. Thanks also to brother Jim for his superb editing.

INTRODUCTION

The gay movement began on the left. Gay Liberation was the third major social eruption, after the civil rights and women's movements, to
emerge out of the dissident political culture of the 1960s. Throughout
the following two decades, as gays developed national organizations,
the movement continued to be tied to the left, although the left itself,
of course, had become decidedly less radical. Like blacks and femi-
nists, gays were natural Democrats. As members of a despised and
even persecuted minority, their interests were represented—if they
were represented at all—by the liberal wing of the Democratic Party.

In the last decade the story has changed dramatically. A significant
number of out homosexuals have broken with the liberal consensus
and declared themselves to be gay conservatives. Indeed, the emergence of gay conservatism as a political and intellectual force is arguably the most important new development in the gay world. At the

level of politics it is most visibly represented by the Log Cabin Republican Club and its leader (until recently), Rich Tafel. Intellectually gay conservatism is represented by the figures I examine in this book.

Let me confess immediately that I am using the term "conservative" in a capacious and perhaps excessively elastic sense. With some justice, two of the figures I discuss, Michelangelo Signorile and Gabriel Rotello, emphatically reject the label. But critics on the gay left have seen important affinities between Signorile and Rotello and self-confessed conservatives like Bruce Bawer and Andrew Sullivan. Essentially I have measured conservatism along three axes. The first and most obvious is politics: gay conservatives repudiate the gay movement's affiliation with the left. The second is gender: gay conservatives seek to rescue homosexuality from its association with gender deviance—with effeminate men and mannish women. And, finally, gay conservatives reject what they consider the sexual license of the Gay Liberation movement and urge gays to restrain their erotic behavior. None of the figures I treat embraces all of these positions without qualification. In fact, much of my attention has gone to identifying the tensions, even contradictions, in their thinking. Yet they share enough ideological ground to justify grouping them together under the label "conservative." Gay radicals, in other words, are not wrong to view them as the common enemy.

The figures I focus on here recommend themselves for study because they have produced the most elaborate and considered arguments for the conservative views they espouse. Although they are all professional journalists, they have found occasion to write books in which they express their ideas in a more expansive and thoughtful fashion than is possible in newspaper columns or op-ed pieces. Their work thus lends itself to the kind of close analytical reading that is my stock-in-trade as an intellectual historian. At the same time, my subjects see themselves as part of a broad-gauged movement within the gay community. In 1996 Bruce Bawer published an anthology of gay conservative writing, *Beyond Queer: Challenging Gay Left Orthodoxy*, which contains contributions from seventeen different authors. Bawer, like Sullivan, views his work as part of "a groundswell for change" or "a new gay paradigm" that marks the homosexual movement's coming of age and shedding of its youthful radicalism.

The new gay conservatism represents a generational shift. All of its adepts were born within a few years of 1960. They are thus a full generation younger than the men and women who authored the Gay Liberation movement—the so-called Stonewall generation. There is more than a hint of Oedipal revolt in their disparaging of the radicalism of their elders, whom they patronize as good-willed but foolish, not heroic pioneers, as the Stonewallers like to see themselves. Significantly, gay conservatism has been a largely male affair. The figures in the movement are nearly all men, and their writings focus heavily on the masculine case. True, Andrew Sullivan makes an effort to include lesbians in his analysis, and one lesbian columnist, Nora Vincent, has made a career of denouncing what she considers the mindless radicalism and terminal dowdiness of lesbian intellectuals. Similarly, in *The Attack Queers: Liberal Media and the Gay Right* Richard Goldstein argues that Camille Paglia is the lesbian counterpart of Andrew Sullivan. While it is true that Paglia and Sullivan constitute a mutual admiration society, and that Paglia is profoundly hostile to queer theory, her thinking is far too idiosyncratic and her politics too leftist (she voted for Ralph Nader in the 2000 election and has been a vocal opponent of the Iraq war) to be called conservative. For the most part, then, gay conservatism is a story about men and by men. Lesbians figure in it, if at all, mainly as foils, whose devotion to domesticity is held up as an example to their libidinous gay brothers. The fact that the new gay conservatism is so resolutely masculine—in personnel and preoccupation—is no doubt significant. The connection between the oppression of women and the oppression of homosexuals was central to the thinking of the Gay Liberation movement. But because women and their problems have been marginalized by gay conservatives, they find it easier to discard the notion that gays are victims of the same patriarchal values that keep women in their place.

I do not mean to suggest that there were no gay conservatives before the generation of Bruce Bawer and Andrew Sullivan declared itself in the 1990s. Obviously there were. The ominous figure of Roy

Cohn (so brilliantly recovered by Tony Kushner in *Angels in America*) comes immediately to mind. But, of course, Cohn was entirely closeted, whereas the defining character of the new generation of conservatives is that they are out and, like their liberal predecessors, make coming out the sine qua non of gay dignity. William Buckley's associate Marvin Liebman represents another kind of forebear. Toward the end of his life Liebman wrote an autobiography, *Coming Out Conservative*, in which he confessed his sexual identity and called on his fellow conservatives to modify their inhumane prejudice on the subject. But Liebman was not a gay conservative in the fashion of Sullivan and Bawer, who are interested less in enlightening right-wingers than in correcting the leftist bias of the gay establishment. Two figures from the 1980s, Larry Kramer and Randy Shilts, are the most important predecessors of the new conservatism: both mounted attacks on gay sexual behavior that anticipated the views of Michelangelo Signorile and Gabriel Rotello. Signorile and Rotello acknowledge Kramer in particular as a major inspiration, and Kramer for his part has embraced them as his ideological heirs. But Kramer and Shilts still considered themselves men of the left. Indeed, Kramer has denounced gay conservatism as a contradiction in terms. So while there are important continuities with the past, the gay conservatism of the 1990s stands out as a distinct and novel development.

* * *

The new gay conservatism has its exact parallel in the black community and, somewhat less perfectly, among women. Figures like Andrew Sullivan and Bruce Bawer are transparently the gay counterparts of black conservatives like Ward Connerly, Shelby Steele, Thomas Sowell, and Clarence Thomas, and they also invite comparison with female conservatives like Phyllis Schafly, Peggy Noonan, Mary Matalin, and Ann Coulter. In the most general sense, the emergence of these conservative intellectuals among constituencies traditionally associated with the left reflects the broad shift of our national politics in a rightward direction over the past quarter century. But a more specific causal logic is at work. Gay conservatism has come into existence, I'm convinced, precisely because of the success of the leftist-inspired Gay Liberation movement that began in the late 1960s. The most fundamental truth about the circumstance of homosexuals in this country is that they have achieved a degree of acceptance that would have been unimaginable at the time of the Stonewall riots in 1969, and that acceptance has been won largely through the labors of the generation of gay activists that emerged out of the Stonewall experience. From this perspective, gay conservatism should be thought of as a luxury that comes with success. Because gays are now so firmly established in the American mainstream, they no longer need to maintain the united ideological front of earlier times. The very same logic accounts for the rise of black conservatism as well.

There is a vulgar Marxist argument—a corollary of the argument from success—that sees gay conservatism as a natural reflection of the economic situation in which most gays find themselves. Typically, so the argument goes, gays are single men and women with double in-comes and no children (DINCS) whose economic circumstances nat-urally incline them to embrace the antitax ideology that has become the centerpiece of the right-wing agenda. Now that homosexuality is widely tolerated, gays no longer have to be concerned about voting their sexual interests and can vote their pocketbooks instead. In other words, only homophobia accounts for the affiliation of gays with the left, and now that its force is diminished they have found their logical home with the supply-siders. Rich Tafel of the Log Cabin Republicans advanced this reasoning when, after the 1994 elections, he argued that more gays had supported the Republicans because the party had toned down its homophobic rhetoric and thus enabled gays to vote their economic interests.

There is reason to be skeptical of this line of reasoning, which in fact has become a staple of antigay propaganda. When gays have de-manded laws to protect them against discrimination, analogous to the laws that protect women and minorities, homophobes have an-swered that they are asking for special rights and that they constitute a privileged class of citizens whose substantial "disposable incomes" place them among the economic elite. In reality, the notion that gays are wealthy is wildly exaggerated. The University of Maryland economist Lee Badgett has shown that gays and lesbians actually make less than their straight counterparts. Nonetheless, it is undoubtedly true that a significant number of well-off gays have succumbed to the logic that their interests are best represented by the right, and they have supplied the new gay conservatism with most of its foot soldiers.

The very success of the gay movement, then, is the main explanation for the rise of gay conservatism. But a factor of nearly equal importance has been the AIDS epidemic. The deradicalizing effect of AIDS is of course most obvious in the chastened sexual behavior it inspired. But I think AIDS also worked in more complex and subtle ways to move gays away from their radical origins. The catastrophe generated an unexpected outpouring of sympathy from straights, and the heroic response of the gay community won it a degree of admiration that contributed significantly to its incorporation into the American mainstream. Virtually all observers of the AIDS epidemic recognize that it has played a key role in the political and cultural integration of gays, and one of the prime effects of that integration has been to wean them from oppositional politics.

Even though the majority of American gays continue to identify with the progressive wing of American politics, one can argue that the new conservatives have exercised an influence on the gay movement far in excess of the number of their actual converts. Since roughly 1990, the issues that have come to dominate gay politics are precisely the issues that gay conservatives put on the table: gay marriage and gays in the military. As Andrew Sullivan and Bruce Bawer and their fellow gay conservatives have argued, the right to marry and the right to serve are profoundly conservative ideas. Above all else, they signal the desire of gays to enter into the most traditional structures of our society, the institutional backbone, one might say, of the social order. Originally viewed with nervous suspicion by the gay establishment and still opposed as profoundly reactionary by gay radicals, they have nonetheless been embraced by the national gay organizations as central objectives of the movement. In a sense, even gay progressives now find themselves fighting for conservative causes—causes that found no place in the original platform of Gay Liberation.

*   *   *

Writing a book about gay conservatives has proved a challenge to my tolerance. Although I believe I have been able to bring a measure of equanimity to the task, I don't delude myself into thinking that my subjects will be pleased with the intellectual portraits I have drawn of them. Still, I found their thinking more complex than I originally anticipated, and I've come to admire the passion and sometimes the rigor with which they argue their case. Mostly, however, I've come to see them as a historical inevitability whose existence, while undeniably irritating, in a curious way offers comforting testimony to the historic progress gays have made over the course of my lifetime. The fact that we now have gay conservatives, one might argue, is the ultimate proof that homophobia is dying.

Conservatives like to present themselves as hard-headed realists who have overcome the fatal sentimentality of liberals. The idea derives from Edmund Burke, who argued that radical efforts to change society ignore the recalcitrance of human emotions and the fragility of social structures. Tinkering with established institutions and beliefs invites totalitarian disaster. The great conservative virtue, in this view, is prudence, which urges tolerating the imperfections of the existing order rather than risking even greater depredations.

I have a certain grudging admiration for the philosophical underpinnings of this outlook. Influenced no doubt by the historical pessimism of Sigmund Freud, I don't find it hard to embrace the rather gloomy estimate of human nature that informs the conservative worldview. But I can't shake the conviction that conservatives overlook the fact that their devotion to prudence has the convenient effect of leaving those who just happen to have wealth and power in the secure possession of their political and economic advantage. In other words, I suspect conservatives of bad faith. They like to see themselves as high-minded and wise defenders of tradition when in reality they are more often grubby advocates for their own material interests.

The gay conservatives I examine in this book can fairly claim to represent the more principled and philosophical impulse in the conservative heritage. I don't see them, as some of their critics do, as abject self-promoters who attack their fellow gays with a view to ingratiating themselves with the straight powers that be. There is, in fact, an almost innocent quality about their polemics. They genuinely believe that in rejecting the teachings of Gay Liberation they are promoting a more enlightened and humane version of homosexuality than that embraced by the generation of gay radicals. If they are guilty of any sin, it is not grubby materialism but a perhaps understandable historical shortsightedness and ingratitude toward the achievements of the men and women of the Stonewall generation who made their very existence possible.

CHAPTER ONE

Bruce Bawer and His Friends

The first manifesto of the new gay conservatism, Marshall Kirk and Hunter Madsen's *After the Ball*, was published in 1989 and quickly became a best seller. The year is significant: it marked the darkest moment in the history of the AIDS epidemic, when the numbers of infected, sick, and dying reached their apogee. The gay community was gripped by what Andrew Holleran has called "the Fear," a collective emotional shutdown in the face of the mounting catastrophe. *After the Ball* should be read, in the first instance, as a response to this moment of high anxiety. Like Randy Shilts's *And the Band Played On: Politics, People, and the AIDS Epidemic*, it is an indictment of the sexual extravagance that the authors believe brought on the epidemic and a call for a dramatic transformation in the behavior and thinking of gay men.

Yet in some respects *After the Ball* is an oddly inappropriate response to the gloomy horror of the disease. Most unnervingly, the authors adopt a jaunty, irreverent tone of voice and offer their remedies in the relentlessly upbeat language of a television infomercial. *After the Ball* is thus light-years removed from the moral earnestness of Bruce Bawer's *A Place at the Table*, with which it shares so much common intellectual ground. Partly, no doubt, their language and tone simply reflect the authors' professional identities: they are neither cultural critics (like Bawer) nor students of political philosophy (like Andrew Sullivan) but a neuropsychiatrist (Kirk) and, significantly, a marketing expert (Madsen). Perhaps they fear being called moralists (as were Randy Shilts, Larry Kramer, and other early critics of gay misbehavior) and hope to deflect the charge by keeping the mood lighthearted, even flippant. But I suspect that the antic rhetorical manner and the addiction to positive thinking are also an unconscious defense mechanism against the terror and depression of the epidemic.

That Kirk and Madsen are involved in a ritual of avoidance is suggested by their actual references to AIDS. Most surprising in a book about homosexuality written in 1989, those references are remarkably few. One might have expected them to hammer away at the morbid consequences of the behavior they decry. But death and disease are kept largely out of sight. Moreover, on the rare occasions the authors do mention the epidemic, they adopt a deliberately hardhearted attitude, untouched by the tragic, not to say lachrymose, sentiment of most AIDS discourse. "AIDS has thinned out the number of eager sexual wantons," they proclaim, almost blithely.

Even more than their language, the basic line of argument they pursue in the book seems willfully superficial. Why must gays change their ways? Not, as Randy Shilts and Larry Kramer argued, because it is a matter of life and death. Not, as Bruce Bawer and Andrew Sullivan will argue, because they are violating moral principles and humane ideals. Rather, they must change, basically, because they are making a bad impression on heterosexuals. Their behavior, in other words, is not so much lethal or reprehensible as it is imprudent. Its main effect is to supply straights with reasons to object to homosexuality and thus to continue discriminating. Hence Kirk and Madsen's central proposal in *After the Ball* is that gays should mount a propaganda campaign—a kind of advertising blitz—that will counteract the association of homosexuality with political radicalism, gender-bending, and sexual excess. By cleaning up their act or, at the very least, cultivating a more presentable and accommodating public image, they will deprive antigay prejudice of its main psychological support. Kirk and Madsen are sure, moreover, that this public relations effort will work: they subtitle their book *How America Will Conquer Its Fear and Hatred of Gays in the '90s*. Their conclusion is as buoyant as their argument is instrumental.

After the Ball aims its criticism at three broad forms of gay malfeasance. The first is the alignment of the gay movement—or of its leaders and organizations—with left-wing political causes. The second is the public display of gender deviance, especially flagrant effeminacy. And the third is the sexual indulgence that became a hallmark of urban gay life in the 1970s. These three will remain the staples of conservative gay criticism throughout the '90s, though the emphasis among them differs, often markedly, from one critic to the next. According to Kirk and Madsen, all three inhibit the cause of gay freedom and equality because they are so offensive to the straight majority. If they can't be eliminated outright, they should at least be restrained and, whenever possible, hidden from view. Only then will gays cease to offend and be accepted by their fellow citizens.

"The gay revolution has failed." The book's opening sentence seems to echo the famous first line of François Furet's *Interpreting the French Revolution*, "The French Revolution is over." In effect Kirk and Madsen call for a gay Thermidor, a repudiation of the radical ideas and practices that initiated the Gay Liberation movement. Storming the barricades of straight society has achieved nothing. Indeed, worse than nothing: the adversarial manner has actually confirmed straights in their homophobia and thus helped perpetuate discrimination. "We're seen by straights as a submicroscopic population of puny freaks, and for us to raise our fists on TV and shout, 'You'd better give us our rights, or else!' can elicit only amusement and disgust." Revolution belongs to the childhood of social movements. Indeed, it is a kind of infantile disorder. Kirk and Madsen call upon gays to grow up and embrace their political maturity. More precisely, they insist that the vast majority of gays in fact already have grown up and adopted appropriately moderate political views. Only the leadership and certain intellectuals remain stuck in their revolutionary infantilism.

The developmental metaphor that associates radicalism with childishness and moderation with maturity is a fixture in the writings of all the new gay conservatives. To a man (and an occasional woman) they demand that the gay movement "come of age" and throw away its revolutionary toys. Indeed, the metaphor is so pervasive that it often seems to substitute for a reasoned discussion of the relative merits of adversarial or accommodating tactics. In the wake of the Reagan Revolution (!) and the fall of Communism, the issue is no longer even debatable. Everyone knows that children rebel while adults negotiate.

The gay movement, then, must renounce all provocative talk of revolution. At the same time, it must not muddy the waters by confusing its goals with those of other political causes. Yet the leaders of the movement, according to Kirk and Madsen, have made just that error. Instead of single-mindedly devoting themselves to advancing gay rights, "Our activists have waltzed from one political issue to the next, publicly committing our movement to solidarity with the Sandinistas, animal protection leagues, migrant farm workers, Trotskyite revolutionaries, the Fat Persons' Liberation Front, the antiapartheid movement, the antinuclear movement, and the Greenpeace Save-the-Whales campaign." Some of these causes may be noble, but they are not gay causes and have no place on the gay agenda. Worse, they create the impression that gays are indiscriminate radicals, which is not only false but tactically harmful. "In the minds of straights," they conclude, "we must be gay people, not leftists."

Like all gay conservatives, Kirk and Madsen seem somewhat embarrassed by their attack on gender nonconformity. Perhaps they recognize that there is more than a whiff of bad faith when a stigmatized minority discriminates against an even smaller minority within its own ranks. They are quick to say that they have no desire to make drag queens, bull dykes, or "other exotic elements of the gay community" feel like second-class queers. Rather, they complain that a constituency representing a small fraction of the gay population figures far too prominently in the public image of homosexuality. They cite evidence from the Kinsey Institute to the effect that only one in seven male homosexuals and one in twenty females exhibit the "telltale" signs of homosexuality. The very rareness of such gender-bending types, they argue, leads Americans to the misconception that few of their fellow citizens are in fact gay—which in turn makes the movement for gay rights seem to be much ado about nothing. Kirk and Madsen are firmly committed to the notion that at least 10 percent of the population is gay, which, they point out, means that there are nearly as many gays as blacks, and three times as many gays as Jews. Eventually, they hope, a citizenry that has learned the truth about homosexuals—namely, that "in all respects other than what we like to do in bed" they are indistinguishable from other Americans—will extend its tolerance even to effeminate men and mannish women. In the meantime, however, smart tactics call for "unconventional-looking gays" to stay "out of the limelight": "Drag queens must understand that the gay stereotype is already heavily skewed in their direction, and that more balance should be achieved by leaning in the opposite direction for a while."

The effeminate and the mannish, then, must delay their gratification. Until the public relations war is won they are urged to tone down their act and keep a low profile. In the meantime, Kirk and Madsen apparently feel comfortable denigrating them in language any homophobe might envy. Thus we encounter, among others, "the prissy young men who staff the fragrance counter at Bloomingdale's," and "a posturing, gesturing, lah-di-da, superannuated prettyboy embalmed in Max Factor cosmetics," as well as middle-aged gays who "come off like sour old biddies." Elsewhere the effeminate and the mannish are virtually equated with child molesters, as when Kirk and Madsen complain, "We call out of the woodwork as our ambassadors of bad will all the screamers, stompers, gender-benders, sado-masochists, and pederasts, and confirm America's worst fears and hates." Apparently the facile pairing of "drag queens and pederasts" causes them no distress; it falls from their lips as readily as salt and pepper or Lewis and Clark.

Effeminacy for Kirk and Madsen is ultimately a product of self-contempt. Because their "naturally feminine appearance and effeminate comportment" can't be hidden, fairies have no choice but to internalize and exaggerate their unmanly identity. Moreover, their "conditioned self-hatred" often spills over into "a hatred of all conventions, and of society in general." In this manner gender deviance gives rise to political radicalism. These unhappy creatures then "fill the ranks of full-time drag queens, the marchers in tutus, the gender-benders and sexual shockers" who do so much damage to the public image of homosexuality.

To counter the impression of homosexuals as gender deviants, Kirk and Madsen propose mounting an advertising campaign—in magazines, on billboards, and TV—featuring self-identified gays and lesbians who are "free of absolutely every element of the widely held stereotypes of how 'faggots' look, dress, and sound." In this way, "prior images of dirty old queens or coarsened dykes" will be replaced by "pleasing new images of all-American and Miss American types." To the criticism that they would be exchanging one stereotype for another, Kirk and Madsen frankly admit that the proposed ads are lies. But, they insist, "it makes no difference that the ads are lies, because we're using them to ethically good effect, to counter negative stereotypes that are every bit as much lies, and far more wicked ones." The "wicked" untruth that gays are effeminate (and lesbians mannish) must be exterminated by whatever means necessary.

After completing their repudiation of effeminacy and spelling out their program for dealing with it, the authors make a startling confession: "One of us, while living, years ago, in an undergraduate dormitory, affected considerable effeminacy." To be specific, he wore cosmetics, bleached and curled his hair, "and baited the more attractive straight boys in the dining room with loud, calculatedly crude taunts and innuendos." Notice that the behavior was merely "affected." It was not the manifestation of a deeply imbedded identity but a set of mannerisms adopted to make an impression. And of course our queenly young author-to-be learned soon enough that the only consequence of his behavior was to alienate potential friends, and he has long since come to regret his "foolishness." Both authors are now firmly committed to butching it up, while keeping the depraved out of sight. Even their prose seems intended to reinforce their masculine image. They speak in the glib, breezy language of sportscasters, with none of the feline languidness of, say, Dorian Gray.

Kirk and Madsen reserve their harshest criticism for the sexual misbehavior of gays. The unsurprising target of their criticism is promiscuity, above all the anonymous promiscuity of the bathhouse and the backroom. They also seem to regard particular sexual act as reprehensible, among them "licking one another's anuses; . . . shoving fists up one anther's rectums; . . . [and] urinating into one anther's mouths." But the main point they wish to make is that "the vast majority of gays" have been unfairly tarnished by the sexual carryings-on of a highly vocal and visible few. As with the matter of effeminacy, in other words, promiscuity and kinkiness are less a real problem than a public relations problem. The majority of gay men, they insist, lead remarkably conventional sex lives: "When it comes to the mechanics of sex, most gays make love the way straights do: with petting, kissing, intercourse, and oral-genital stimulation." That the "intercourse" in question is anal intercourse they prefer to leave unsaid, for it not only distinguishes gay sex from straight sex but also brings to mind such unsavory acts as rimming and fisting.

Kirk and Madsen don't say how they know that most homosexuals are innocent of the "grossest, kinkiest" practices engaged in by gay libertines. One might counter that the huge market in gay pornography suggests that even if those practices are as rare as our authors believe, they play a significant role in the gay erotic imagination. But Kirk and Madsen are less concerned with actual behavior than with the widespread perception among straights that gay men are sexual addicts. The perception is particularly disastrous in America, with its deep puritanical prejudice about "the naughtiness of sex." Hence their proposed advertising campaign would strip homosexuality of any hint of eroticism: "The imagery of sex per se should be downplayed, and the issue of gay rights reduced, as far as possible, to an abstract social question." In other words, because the popular perception of gays has been oversexualized, the public relations offensive must counter with the opposite exaggeration, namely, that gayness has virtually nothing to do with sex. Above all, it must stress that gays cherish the same romantic ideals as straights: "We're not fighting for the right to suck and fuck, in full public view, with as many one-minute stands as we can possibly line up end to end, until our mouths and anuses are sore and we're all dying of syphilis and AIDS. We're fighting for the right to love and marry, not merely to blast away with our 'hot love-guns.'" The denigration of "sucking and fucking" and the proclivity for what I call "love talk" are signature features of all the gay conservatives who follow in Kirk and Madsen's wake. A sentimental romanticism replaces Gay Liberation's full-throated commitment to sexual pleasure. The new gay citizen they hope to present to the public is moderate, manly, and chaste.

II

Bruce Bawer's *A Place at the Table*, published in 1993, revisits the themes addressed by Kirk and Madsen in *After the Ball* but in a categorically more thoughtful and serious frame of mind. A poet and literary critic, Bawer made a name for himself in the 1980s reviewing movies in the *American Spectator*. His book advances the principal ideas that have come to dominate gay conservative thought. It insists that homosexuality has nothing to do with any political agenda and thus aims to sever the historic ties between the gay movement and the left. It also denies that gayness involves a rejection of traditional gender roles—effeminate men and mannish women. And it disputes the association of homosexuality with sexual license, arguing that most gays, like most straights, long for romantic monogamy and, ultimately, marriage.

Bawer doesn't call himself a conservative. On the contrary, he says that he is a Democrat and politically to the left of most gay Americans. And, in fact, *A Place at the Table* does not expressly endorse the policies we associate with modern American conservatism—lower taxes, less government, ending affirmative action, and the like. Bawer may well favor such policies (one suspects he does), but he wisely says nothing about them in the book, because to do so would weaken the force of his basic contention that homosexuality has no ideological implications—that it is "a simple, morally neutral, and intrinsically uninteresting truth" without any necessary consequences for one's views about politics, culture, or religion.

Bawer's central complaint in *A Place at the Table* is that the movement for homosexual rights has been hijacked by radicals. To be sure, he acknowledges the historical debt of the modern gay movement to the rebels of the 1960s, immediately to the drag queens who challenged the police at New York's Stonewall Inn in 1969, and to the counterculture more generally. "Let it be said," he concedes, "that for all the vanity and imprudence that many of us associate with 1960s culture and politics, the decade's emancipatory atmosphere encouraged homosexuals to stand up for themselves as never before. Indeed, it is hard to imagine a large-scale gay-rights movement springing to life in less reckless times, for, before the movement began to change things, saying 'I'm homosexual' in public *was* an almost insanely reckless thing to do." So radicalism was necessary to the birth of Gay Liberation, just as it was to the civil rights movement and the women's movement. But it was a regrettable necessity that soon outgrew its usefulness. Like a guest invited to stay the night who moves in for good, radicals retained their stranglehold on gay opinion and politics long after they had performed their historical function, and as a result the movement has become more and more irrelevant to the actual lives of gay men and women.

The particular object of Bawer's disdain is the ideal of "alliance politics" embraced, he argues, by the gay establishment and its intellectual spokesmen. The advocates of alliance politics believe that the oppression of gays is intrinsically linked to the oppression of other groups in society, above all women and minorities. They see deep structural ties, in other words, between homophobia, sexism, and racism. In their bolder moments (which have grown rarer as capitalism has secured its hold on the Western political imagination), they extend the structural link to include economic inequality: full gay liberation requires not only the liberation of women and racial minorities but also the overcoming of poverty. In its more modest or tactical guise, alliance politics argues merely that, as a small and despised population, gays need to combine forces with other disadvantaged constituencies.

Bawer denies that the interests of homosexuals have any connection to those of such other groups. Individual gay men and women might of course choose to fight sexism, racism, and even capitalism, but there is no reason why the gay movement as such should embrace these causes, or any other. In Bawer's view, the movement's leaders have arbitrarily imposed their own ideological convictions on an enterprise that ought to have the sole objective of securing the freedom and equality of homosexuals. "The moderate gay rights movement is, quite simply, about gay rights. By contrast, gay-left leaders apparently view those rights as only one plank of a comprehensive socialist platform that all gays are inherently obliged to support." The experienced polemicist obviously enjoys smearing alliance politics with the label "socialist"—even though among prominent American gays perhaps only Tony Kushner qualifies as a socialist—just as he enjoys exaggerating the idea of a structural affinity between gays and other disadvantaged groups into the totalitarian proposition that all homosexuals are "inherently obliged" to support such a platform. By the same logic Bawer objects to broadening the movement for homosexual rights to include transsexuals, whose plight has no innate connection with that of gays because, he says, most of them are heterosexual. Gender deviance, in other words, is simply not a gay issue.

A Place at the Table contends that the political and sexual radicals who dominate the gay movement and are so visible in gay culture in fact represent a small minority of the gay population. Hence, despite their supposed prominence and power, Bawer always refers to them as "subculture" gays, implying that they are both few in number and wedded to eccentric ideas and practices, rather like hippies or survivalists. They have little in common with the vast majority of homosexuals, who just "want to lead open, ordinary middle-class lives" and whose views and conduct, save in the matter of sexual orientation, are indistinguishable from the American mainstream. He cites no sociological studies to support this analysis, and one often has the feeling that he has projected his own experiences and desires into a tendentious opposition between a large gay majority that is silent and virtuous and a small minority that misbehaves noisily. No one could object had he argued merely that, as a result of the very success of the gay movement, larger numbers of conservative gays are now coming out of the closet, or that the emergence of a more conventional homosexuality has been among the most remarkable developments of the past decade. But, invoking only anecdotal evidence (most of it personal), he insists on the more extreme formulation, which pits a "marginal" but "obtrusive" subculture that monopolizes gay organizations and public display against the "millions" of homosexuals who embrace middle-of-the-road politics, conform to society's gender expectations, and accept a code of sexual conduct little different from their straight counterparts.

Complementing this notion of a radical few who misrepresent the conventional many is a second trope deployed throughout the book. Bawer suggests there is a kind of ideological equivalence between gay activists on the left and Christian homophobes on the right. He denies that they are *moral* equivalents: even the "most shrill and obnoxious" activists are preferable to homophobes, however genteel. But he nonetheless insists that the two groups are mirror images of one another. "The rhetorical battlefield," he writes in a typical passage, "has sometimes appeared to be occupied almost exclusively by extremist demagogues—by far-right fundamentalist superpatriots without an ounce of Christian charity or respect for American liberties, and by radical gay activists who respond to antigay attacks by issuing wholesale condemnations of capitalism and Christianity." Andrew Sullivan is fond of the same pairing. He often complains that the debate over homosexuality has been monopolized by "paleoconservatives" on the one side and "paleoradicals" on the other, both of whom he considers ideological Neanderthals.

Bawer's hostility to gay activists does not end with his indictment of their doctrinaire politics and sexual extravagance. He finds their behavior so irrational and offensive that it begs us to imagine darker (and largely unconscious) motives. Sounding curiously like a vulgar Marxist, he suggests that some radicals—notably members of ACT UP—are enraged because queerness has disrupted their comfortable, bourgeois existences. "All their lives," he writes, "they've taken for granted their health, prosperity, and privilege, and their own homosexuality is the first curve ball that life has thrown them." For others, gay radicalism is at bottom a manifestation of self-contempt. Groups like the Lesbian Avengers or Queer Nation "don't really take themselves—or anything—seriously, especially where sex is concerned"; "many of them have never really liberated themselves from their parents' view of homosexuality as a joke." The charge that activists suffer from internalized homophobia is nothing if not ingenious, because it allows Bawer to turn the tables on his critics, who like to say that gay conservatives are basically self-hating. Somewhat fancifully, he also proposes that radical activism is often a replacement for the promiscuous sex that AIDS has forced the activists to abandon: "It is ecstatic, irrational, existential, orgasmic; indeed, I have often felt that for those with powerful memories of long-ago encounters in parks and bathhouses, . . . such activism serves as a substitute for self-destructive promiscuous sex." So gay radicals are disgruntled yuppies given to self-hatred and addicted to a kind of ersatz hedonism.

If asked how a small number of political and sexual radicals have managed to wrest control of the gay movement and dominate the public image of homosexuality, Bawer's answer is that it is actually the fault of the silent majority of gays, including his former self. The radicals have prevailed because, until very recently, conservative gays remained closeted and thus invisible. In effect, they ceded the movement, and along with it control over society's perception of homosexuality, to the radicals. Accordingly, the centerpiece of Bawer's prescription for a more reasonable gay politics is that everyone must come out. "The best way . . . to counter the heinous, large-scale disinformation campaigns by anti-gay crusaders is to come out *now*." It is a prescription he shares with all the new gay conservatives. And of course it is a prescription that alienates him from his straight allies on the right, who think that homosexuals, at the very least, should be discreet about their misfortune.

Bawer's devotion to coming out is not as categorical as some of his statements (like the one I just cited) imply. He has a hard time drawing the line between an appropriate candor and the kind of flaunting of one's sexuality he deplores in Gay Pride parades. "Civilization relies on a certain degree of restraint," he intones, and the indiscriminate advertising of one's sexual orientation in public demonstrations reflects "a lamentable antagonism toward the value of privacy, toward the idea of propriety, and toward the notion that life should be divided into private and public realms." Even with friends and family the decision to come out needs to be carefully monitored, since it can so easily degenerate into "narcissistic display." He also warns against coming out before you are emotionally ready, citing the example of a college friend who broadcasted his gayness and then committed suicide when his mentor cut him off. "It made me realize," Bawer concludes, "that the compulsion to announce one's homosexuality at an early stage of one's sexual self-awareness can . . . be the manifestation of a terrible vulnerability, insecurity, and sense of guilt about being gay." Arguably such pronouncements show an admirable sensitivity to the ambiguities of coming out. But they can also be read as betraying lingering feelings of shame about homosexuality. Bawer further reports his dissatisfaction with the coming-out scenes in gay novels, because they wrongly imply that sexual orientation is "a Big Deal," when, as we've seen, it is for him "a simple, morally neutral, and intrinsically uninteresting truth." Underlying his squeamishness about coming out—in spite of his belief in its moral correctness and political necessity—one senses a desire to keep sex in its place. He offers the paradoxical spectacle of a self-declared homosexual who has little enthusiasm for the erotic.

Just as homosexuality has no implications for politics, it also has no implications for religion. Bawer views the antagonism between gays and Christians as an artifact of the same perverse dialectic that has created the unnatural alliance of homosexuality and radicalism. On the one side, Christian authorities, especially fundamentalists, cite scripture to argue that homosexuality is an abomination, while, on the other side, gay activists respond to this incitement by denouncing religion tout court. Bawer recounts his own religious history to illustrate the process. He was brought up a Christian and said his bedtime prayers, he reports, "right up until the night before the day that I realized I was gay." His religious reading and Sunday school lessons had persuaded him that a Christian could take only one attitude toward homosexuality, namely, that it was sinful. So when, at twenty, he finally recognized his sexual identity, he had no choice, he felt, but to reject Christ, which he did for ten years. He overcame the conviction that Christianity and homosexuality are incompatible and returned to the faith of his childhood only after he began going to church with his lover and when he read John Boswell's *Christianity, Social Tolerance, and Homosexuality*, which for him demolished the scriptural arguments against homosexuality. Andrew Sullivan, who is a serious Roman Catholic, makes an almost identical argument about Christianity and homosexuality in *Virtually Normal*, though his relations to orthodoxy remain more troubled than Bawer's.

Bawer's analysis of the homosexual predicament is conceptually grounded in his essentialism and his radical individualism. During the past two decades gay intellectuals have argued over whether homosexuality is a naturally occurring condition, rooted in biology, or a socially constructed, historically contingent identity that has come into existence only in the last century. Although both views can be used to support homophile politics, social constructionism is the favored perspective on the left, especially among queer theorists. For one thing, it is less abject than essentialism, which seems to imply that homosexuality should be tolerated mainly because it is involuntary. For another, it carries the possibility that the number of homosexuals may increase, for if gay identity is a function of society and history, friendlier social and historical circumstances could encourage more individuals to embrace it.

Given the history of this debate and its ideological valence, we should not be surprised that Bawer, like all the gay conservatives, is a resolute essentialist. He believes that homosexuality is deeply embedded in the psyche, perhaps even the body. "The truth is," he writes, "sexual orientation comes from inside. It's probably entirely innate," a manifestation of "biological urges." He mentions approvingly Dean Hamer's study that pretends to show a connection between homosexuality and certain genetic markers, a study that is broadly derided by constructionists but that for Bawer "add[s] to the growing body of evidence that sexual orientation is hereditary." Accordingly, he dismisses as preposterous, even "obscene," the notion that homosexuality can be chosen—and hence also abandoned: "A homosexual man can no more stop being homosexual than a black can cease being black." His immediate target here is homophobes on the right, who invoke the supposedly voluntary character of homosexuality as an excuse to discriminate. But he is just as hostile to constructionists on the left—he mentions John D'Emilio and Donna Minkowitz—who say there are more gays now than in the past and who hope their numbers will continue to grow.

Doubtless Bawer's essentialist convictions are an authentic reflection of his own experience. Homosexuality, he says, can't be a matter of preference "because it doesn't *feel* like a preference." But in treating it as a biological fluke that occurs independently of culture or society he also strengthens his contention that sexual orientation is "morally neutral and without interest." As a random accident of nature, it can be the object of neither rebuke nor celebration. Homophobes and gay radicals are both wrong to saddle it with profound moral significance. In reality it is as inconsequential as being left-handed or blue-eyed. He is thus no more sympathetic to the progressive cry that "Gay is good" than to the reactionary one that it is evil. "It is neither good nor evil. It simply *is*." In this manner his essentialism contributes subtly to his campaign to belittle the human importance of sexuality—to establish that it is no "Big Deal." Only homophobia can explain how something so trivial could have taken on earth-shaking significance—and forced Bruce Bawer to write a whole book about it.

Precisely because it is a naturally occurring, probably genetic, phenomenon, homosexuality for Bawer is also radically individual. He rejects the idea that gays form a community or, even worse, a "brotherhood," with a shared culture or sensibility. Rather, the community of homosexuals has only a strategic rationale: it has been created by homophobia and has as its sole justification the fight against discrimination. When that fight is won, the community will have lost its raison d'être and wither away. Without homophobia "gays would still gravitate to each other because of sexual or romantic attraction, but there would be nothing to bind homosexuals together en masse in gay bars or restaurants, gay churches or synagogues, or Gay Studies programs." The notion of gay solidarity was always specious anyway, as gays treat each other with the same ruthless selfishness as straights, especially in bars, where "the beautiful and the moneyed tend to get what they want, and God help the rest." But even where it is not specious, it is lamentable, because it fosters the wrongheaded—and ultimately totalitarian—notion that a common sexual orientation brings with it shared ideas and values and feelings of identification. For many gay activists, of course, the sense of community is itself as valuable as the political goals it is meant to foster. But for Bawer it is merely oppressive. It creates the bogus notion that sexual orientation has necessary consequences for one's politics, religion, tastes, gender style, or even sex life, when by rights all these are properly autonomous. In his robust individualism Bawer is of course typical of modern conservatives, who are heirs to nineteenth-century European liberalism and largely innocent of any Burkean sense of community. Significantly, the subtitle of his book is *The Gay Individual in American Society*.

III

Bawer prefers his homosexuals invisible. They should declare their sexual orientation, certainly, but in appearance and demeanor they ought to be indistinguishable from their brothers and sisters of the straight persuasion. *A Place at the Table* has as a central objective separating homosexuality from gender deviance—from the over-wrought masculinity of leathermen and bull dykes and, even more, from the flamboyant effeminacy of drag queens and their nelly imita-tors. Perhaps because he's aware that his dislike of effeminacy iden-tifies him with traditional straight prejudice—and thus puts him in the awkward position of seeming to endorse discrimination—he is often less than forthright about his aversion. He prefers to talk of "gestures and mannerisms" and "ways of speaking and walking," or he insists, lamely, that it is not effeminacy per se but its exaggeration to which he objects: "I don't hate seeing people in leather or drag; what I hate is the thought that to some of them, the leather or drag is the cornerstone of their identity." Nevertheless one gets the firm impression that we would be better off without "shrill, effeminate" men and "stomping macho" lesbians.

For Bawer such departures from society's expectations about how men and women should deport themselves have no intrinsic con-nection to homosexuality. Unlike same-sex desire, which, as we've seen, he believes is inborn and hence essential, effeminacy and man-nishness are for him social constructions (though he doesn't use the phrase). To be precise, they are "manifestations of institution-alized prejudice," stereotypical responses to homophobia. He doesn't offer a systematic or historically informed argument about how gender-bending might have emerged as a defense mechanism against homophobia, but there is no question that he considers it such. Fun-damentally it is a pathology, a cry of pain, which we can expect to disappear when homophobia itself disappears. Freed from their in-ternal demons, gay men and lesbians will be restored to their natural masculinity and femininity. In the meantime, leathermen and drag queens are wrongly celebrated as icons of Gay Liberation. Rather, they are unhappy relics of oppression.

Gay men have long been divided in their feelings about effemi-nacy. Many of them—perhaps the majority—harbor the same preju-dice against "flamers" as do straights. At some level they may be aware of a contradiction between their apology for homosexuality and their condescension toward gays who are visibly unmanly. But, like Bawer, they think effeminate behavior fosters the stereotypical notion that gay men really want to be women and that it thereby impedes the acceptance of gays by straight society. On the other hand, a significant minority of gays hold that gay liberation should be as much about liberating gender as it is about the right to same-sex romance. At a theoretical level they even argue that homophobia is rooted in prejudice against women: hatred of gays reflects our society's deep contempt for the feminine, and it will not end until this misogyny is overcome. Gays who bash sissies thus unwittingly betray their own interests.

Bawer gives no indication that he has ever thought about a possible connection between gay oppression and the oppression of women. On the contrary, as we've seen, he expressly denies that gays as such have any obligation to battle misogyny, just as they have no obligation to battle racism. Nor does he appreciate that for some gays the right to adopt an unpopular gender style is as essential to their sense of self as is his own need to love men. Or to the extent he recognizes that such folks exist he finds them regrettable, and he insists their fate is not a proper concern for the homosexual rights movement. He thus finds himself in the ironic position of arguing, at least implicitly, that the sole common denominator among gays is same-sex desire—"ironic" because he elsewhere denounces radical activists for reducing gays to their sexuality.

Bawer's hostility to effeminacy is, one suspects, the main reason he dislikes Gay Pride parades. To be sure, he is bothered by the overt sexuality of many of the marchers: men in underwear, bare-breasted women, couples who "kiss or grab each other's crotches or rub their bodies together in a simulation of sex." He also objects strenuously that the members of NAMBLA, the North American Man-Boy Love Association, are allowed to march and thus to propagate the lie that homosexuals advocate pedophilia. (He reserves a special place in his pantheon of shame for Allen Ginsberg, who "sold himself as a gay laureate only to behave like a vulgar oaf, shedding his clothes in public and rhapsodizing about sex with minors.") But what most irritates Bauer in Gay Pride demonstrations, one senses, is the public display of men behaving like women. Of the 1992 New York parade he writes,

"There was more sashaying and queeny posing in a couple of hours than one could expect to see in a solid month of bar-hopping." The "grotesque appearance and vulgar behavior" of the marchers represent "a public-relations nightmare," not least because they provide the radical right with invaluable footage for propaganda videos like "The Gay Agenda."

Bawer wants homosexuals to be not just manly but positively buttoned-down. The ACT UP protesters at the 1992 Republican convention, in his view, "should have been . . . looking every bit as clean-cut and wholesome as the Republican Youth Coalition members." In happy contrast to the scruffy protesters, the gay men who attend his church are all "elegantly turned out in a suit and tie and polished black shoes." From his own observation he also reports that the effeminacy and overt sexuality of Gay Pride marchers invariably offend straight viewers. "In every instance," he writes, "I saw nothing on their faces but shock, revulsion, and desperate desire to get away from Fifth Avenue as quickly as possible." One suspects Bawer saw what he wanted to see. From my own experience I would have said that straight viewers are as apt to be exhilarated or amused as incensed.

Closely related to his dislike of effeminacy is his aversion to the notion of a gay sensibility or gay style. Here again he finds a confusion of the essential and the contingent. Historically gays have indeed been drawn to certain cultural forms, like Broadway musicals and opera, as well as certain artists and performers. "It *is* true," he concedes, "that from an early age, often long before he realizes that he is gay, many a homosexual will find himself amused by certain movies or touched by certain songs or captivated by certain female performers that may not interest his heterosexual friends." Bawer himself is no exception: his other writing reveal a vast familiarity with American musical theater, though he prides himself that, in contrast to the stereotypical gay man, he has no use for opera. These affinities, like gender nonconformity, result from oppression; they serve as a kind of palliative for egos damaged by homophobia. He speculates, plausibly, that gay icons like Bette Davis or Billy Holiday perform this function by satirizing the heterosexual conventions from which gays are excluded. But the days of the opera queen and the movie queen are numbered. As artifacts of homophobia, they too will fall into desuetude (and their hothouse nature will be revealed) as more and more gays come out of the closet.

While effeminacy is an irritant, it can't compete for Bawer's disapproval with promiscuity, which he discusses at greater length and with more vehemence than any other evil of contemporary homosexuality. Once more he accuses gay radicals of confounding two entirely separate matters: the struggle for gay rights and the issue of sexual freedom. There is simply no logical connection between the demand that gays should enjoy the same right to erotic fulfillment as straights and the demand that they be allowed—indeed encouraged—to pursue an unlimited number of partners, many of them anonymous. Yet the leaders of the movement, especially in the 1970s, made just that equation, even though, according to Bawer, the vast majority of gays wanted only to be permitted to fall in love and settle down with their mates. Instead of seeking to pass laws that would have secured such relationships—domestic partnership legislation—"the most visible gay activists of the 1970s and early '80s made almost a sacred cause out of the right of gay men to anonymous and promiscuous gay sex." More than a right, promiscuity became an obligation. Fidelity was denounced as a straight bourgeois hang-up; gays realized their true identity only when they overcame it.

Bawer finds evidence for this doctrine in the writings of three prominent gay novelists of the 1970s and 1980s, Edmund White, Andrew Holleran, and Paul Monette. Edmund White's *States of Desire* is especially hateful to him. Written on the eve of the AIDS epidemic, the book recounts White's travels across gay America and cheerfully endorses the sexual adventuring he finds in backrooms and bathhouses. Bawer objects not just to the endorsement but to White's argument that gay promiscuity represents a triumph over the limitations of heterosexual monogamy: "He ridicules the 'self-hatred' of gays who 'pair off' into permanent couples. Gay Lib, he asserts, has moved past 'love' into a Brave New World in which promiscuity vanquishes possessiveness and jealousy." Bawer does not bother to engage with White's case for promiscuity; its ludicrousness is taken to be self-evident. He merely notes that the book "glorifies" a way of life that brought us AIDS.

Neither Andrew Holleran nor Paul Monette offers as fat a target as Edmund White, who, at the very least, can be accused of bad timing. He objects to Holleran's "Notes on Promiscuity" not because Holleran champions promiscuity (which he doesn't) but because he treats it with ironic detachment, as if it were (to use Bawer's own phrase) no big deal. He criticizes Holleran's great novel of the 1970s, *Dancer from the Dance*, for setting up a false dichotomy between gays who are "out, proud, and promiscuous" and those who are "closeted, ashamed, and repressed." The characterization is not inaccurate, but it fails to do justice to the undertone of melancholy that makes Holleran's portrait of gay disco culture so unforgettable. A similar flatfootedness mars Bawer's treatment of Paul Monette's autobiography, *Becoming a Man*, in which, he says, Monette "comes across as a stereotype of the promiscuous gay man who serves up pretentious rhetoric about 'existential sexuality.' " I find no mention of "existential sexuality" in the book, and Monette's erotic adventures (many of which were with women) are more mocked than celebrated. His central theme is the search for "the laughing man" who will become his life's companion—in other words, just the sort of romantic object that Bawer himself recommends. A more forthright defender of promiscuity is the lesbian writer Donna Minkowitz, who praises gays for "solving the problem that has kept heterosexuals sad for centuries—how to combine emotional fidelity with sexual freedom." But Bawer will have none of it. "Minkowitz to the contrary," he writes, "the huge majority of [gays] don't want to be defiant, promiscuous East Village radicals; they don't want to teach the world how to have better sex. They just want to be able to love in the way that comes naturally to them, in the places where they feel at home."

Bawer will not allow that promiscuity has any natural attractions. He argues, improbably, that gays became promiscuous in the 1970s only because they were talked into it. Desire had nothing to do with it—or at least very little compared with the propaganda emanating from the gay left. Promiscuity, in this analysis, was virtually a creation of the subculture. He illustrates the process of seduction from his own life: "When I first came out to a gay friend in the early 1980s, AIDS was already in the news and the dangers of anonymous sex almost universally recognized, but that didn't prevent my friend from giving me the standard gay-subculture advice—to go to a bathhouse. I hadn't expressed any interest in having anonymous sex, . . . but that didn't matter: in the gay subculture, bathhouse sex was an essential rite of passage; you *needed* to sleep with a lot of strangers—so the theory ran—in order to grow accustomed to the idea of homosexuality and to know and like and accept yourself as a gay person. So it is that many young homosexuals become promiscuous not because they really want to but because they are encouraged to believe that that's what one does, what one *must* do, when one is gay." Andrew Sullivan, as we'll see, is willing to acknowledge the genuine appeal of promiscuity, even though he struggles to resist it. But for Bawer the temptation is apparently so mild that only proselytizing can explain why a generation of gay men succumbed to it.

Frank Browning, the author of *The Culture of Desire: Paradox and Perversity in Gay Lives Today* (1993)—which defends the centrality of sex in gay life—has called Bawer "sex-negative." If "sex-negative" means taking as dim a view of sex as, say, the ancient fathers of the desert, the charge is unfair. After all, you can't write a book defending the right of gays to freedom and equality without implicitly affirming that sexual desire has its legitimate claims. But most of Bawer's energy in *A Place at the Table* goes into circumscribing those claims. He objects to the way radical activists have made sex the defining element of gay identity, when in fact it is "*only* a part" of the picture. "Being gay," he insists, "is not about sex as such. Fundamentally, it's about one's core emotional identity." By itself sexual experience has no value, just as pleasure has no autonomous rationale. It becomes legitimate only when it is bound by love—by a deep, sustained, and singular emotional attachment to another human being. Loosed from such an attachment, it is "dehumanizing," "mechanical," "impersonal," "sheer animal gratification," "even bestial." Bawer, in other words, is a strict romantic monogamist. He has little tolerance for the idea that sexual pleasure might be a good thing in its own right, and even less for the contention of sex radicals that it is integral to their sense of meaning and identity.

Whether or not these views make Bawer "sex-negative," they certainly limit the importance of erotic experience and diminish its charms. His fundamental unease with sex is evident in his reaction to the photograph on the cover of Frank Browning's *Culture of Desire*. He has nothing to say about Browning's argument, which one might have expected him to dispute. But the photo inspires a sustained outburst: "The picture jolted me, for it seemed to reflect a determination to reinforce all the negative stereotypes about homosexuality. It showed two bare-chested young men who were at most twenty-five years old. They stood one behind the other, directly facing the camera. The one in front was something out of a sex fantasy: blond and beautiful, with a perfectly developed upper body, he stood with his legs apart, his jeans unbuckled, and the top of his underwear showing, Marky Mark–style. He was centered directly on the spine, so that when you placed the book on a shelf with your other books you could see him among the staid titles, face and navel and crotch. . . . His partner, standing behind him, . . . looked disturbed, psychotic. There was the slightest suggestion of danger—one could easily imagine him tightening his grip around his beautiful partner's neck and choking him to death." The reaction is so over-the-top, even empirically mistaken, that it makes one wonder what dark urges might be festering in Bawer's sexual imagination. The boy in front is clearly not blond but brunette. And only a hyperactive fantasy could transform his partner into a murderer. For all we know, they are just two young men in love. But in Bawer's mind the photo "reinforces the stereotypical equation of homosexuality with lewdness and promiscuity."

Bawer defends himself against Frank Browning's charge in an essay, "Sex-Negative Me," published in the *Advocate* of 23 August 1994. Here he adopts a more indulgent tone. For gays, he says, "sex can be anything from casual fun to a fundamental component of a loving, committed relationship." So far as I know, it is the only time he admits that sex might be fun. Yet in the same piece he also rails against

THE
CULTURE
OF
DESIRE

FRANK
BROWNING

those who equate gay sex with animal coupling, while straight sex is considered "an integral part of the complex web of human feeling, connectedness, and commitment before God." He clearly hates being called a prude, but he can't avoid leaving the impression that sex makes him queasy if it is not romantically insulated.

Naturally Bawer is a proponent of gay marriage, although he is less adamant about legalization than is Andrew Sullivan, who argues that the right to marry and to join the military should be the only planks in the gay platform. "Call them what you will, marriages or domestic partnerships or whatever," writes Bawer, "the point is acknowledging and endorsing them, rather than rejecting and discouraging them, would be a socially positive act, conservative in the best sense of the word." Marriage is conservative because it makes workers more reliable and homes more stable. The state thus has a natural interest in encouraging homosexuals to live together as couples rather than alone and sleeping around. But Bawer defends gay marriage less on the grounds of its social utility than because of its emotional satisfactions. Above all, it gives gays what all human beings most desire in life, namely, a family—and, under the best of circumstances, even an enriched bond to their families of birth. He charts the process in his own experience: "For years my life as a gay person was something that existed utterly apart from my life with my family and straight friends. For the most part, that gay life, such as it was, took place three or four evenings a month, in and around the gay bars where I would drink, chat with friends, and watch music videos for a few hours. At the time, I couldn't imagine the two lives ever becoming one; and so it was remarkable to me, after I met and fell in love with and eventually moved in with Chris, to watch my life as a gay person become a part of my other life—to see this man whom I'd met in a bar become a member of my family and to see myself become a member of his." Presumably his days of drinking, chatting, and watching music videos in gay bars also included having sex, though the elision is telling. His point, however, is that the satisfactions of a single gay life pale beside those of being in love and sharing a home: "Life without a home—a home that is centered on a strong and stable loving relationship—seemed to both of us an empty, meaningless prospect." Nothing pleases him more than when his straight friends acknowledge the relationship and indicate that they accept it as identical in every emotional sense to their own relationships. And nothing angers him more than any slight that implies a lack of such parity, as, for example, when, at the wedding of two straight friends, marriage between a man and a woman was pronounced "the only foundation for an enduring home." Interestingly, he says nothing about the desirability of children in such a home. Indeed, he got into a wrangle with the reviewer of his book in the *New York Times* when she opined that society legitimately privileges straight marriages because they "are oriented toward the generation and rearing of children." Bawer countered that by such reasoning infertile heterosexuals should also not be allowed to marry. But logically one would expect him to welcome the "Gayby Boom" of the past decade, since it enhances the importance of family for gays and strengthens their conservative credentials.

IV

Readers will have discerned that *A Place at the Table* is a highly autobiographical book. Indeed, it is as much an autobiography as an ideological tract. Or, perhaps more accurately, its argument for gay conservatism is supported mainly by evidence from Bawer's own experience. In many ways, this autobiographical manner is one of the book's most attractive features—and makes it a more effective piece of advocacy than the impersonal jeremiads of Marshall Kirk and Hunter Madsen in *After the Ball*. We never doubt the depth or genuineness of his convictions. Even his humorlessness comes as a relief after the jokey superficiality of Kirk and Madsen. But the disadvantage of relying so heavily on autobiography is the naïve assumption that his case is representative—that he speaks for "the silent majority" of gay Americans. As Joan Scott reminds us, the evidence of experience is an unreliable guide to history, and sometimes even to the real meaning of the experience itself.

Bawer might almost be said to have inherited his conservatism. Like many children, he automatically embraced the political and religious views of his traditional-minded parents. As he says himself, "I was a baby conservative." Perhaps because they were so admirable and loving, his identification with his parents was unusually intense. He seems even to have outdone them in rectitude. By his own confession, he was "moralistic to the point of being a pain in the neck," and he recounts several amusing instances of his exaggerated scrupulousness. His critics would doubtless maintain that the stuffy moralism of the child still afflicts the adult. Yet the universal testimony of everyone who knew him agrees, he says, that he was "an unusually kind and considerate boy."

Kind and considerate, that is, until he was "threatened by the possibility of sexual self-knowledge," as happened in the eighth grade when a quiet, gentle classmate became "the chief object" of his affection. One day in the schoolyard, to impress his rowdier peers, he found himself calling the boy a "faggot." At the time he had no awareness of his motive or even apparently of the word's meaning. Later, however, he came to see it as an act of unconscious projection: "Terrified by my affection for Paul, I had attached to him the label—'faggot'—that I had never consciously affixed to myself but that I subconsciously dreaded might apply to me." He doesn't say that the word connoted sexual desire to him (even though, as an eighth-grader, he must have known about desire). Rather, he speaks of his feelings for the boy in the erotically more anodyne language of "affection" and "spiritual kinship." What the word in fact marked was a rudimentary gender distinction: the chosen friend was "quiet" and "gentle," while the boys he wished to impress were "rowdy." "Faggot" in other words meant—or at least hinted at—effeminacy.

Throughout his childhood and adolescence, moreover, effeminacy, rather than same-sex desire, was the primary association he had with homosexuality and the reason he could not imagine himself as a homosexual. He was "a perfectly ordinary boy," attractive to girls, with nothing in his "manner" to suggest he might be gay. Homosexuals, by contrast, were "flamboyant, sissyish creatures with lisps and limp wrists." He felt absolutely nothing in common with "grotesque characters" known to be homosexual like Liberace or Truman Capote or with his one "flagrantly gay" high-school classmate, who was "fat and effeminate and quip-happy." Homosexuals liked to cook and sew and gossip. They were, in short, men who wanted to be women.

Although he couldn't think of himself as homosexual, because it connoted loathsome effeminacy, he nonetheless recognized that he was different from other adolescents. Most important, he did not share their growing interest in girls. Instead he found himself "preoccupied" with certain boys, separation from whom during summer vacations left him upset and dispirited. At some level he knew that his feelings were sexual: to make sense of them he "secretly read every word" about adolescent sexuality in his physician-father's "extensive" library of medical books. But all his interpretive energy went into persuading himself that the real source of his interest in boys was something more innocent than lust. Thus he theorized that what appeared to be sexual attraction was just an exaggerated manifestation of his perfectly natural feelings of friendship. Or perhaps it merely disguised his envy of the boys' looks and poise, a reflection of his own insecurity. Or he surmised that the attraction was not really erotic but aesthetic: he was "an admirer of beauty," and admiring the beauty of another boy was no different from admiring a work of literature or art or music. Bawer is generally tolerant of his adolescent self, but he views all these theories as patent rationalizations.

He presents one further hypothesis that readers of his book are bound to find much more intriguing than his flimsy ideas about friendship, envy, and beauty. "I had another theory," he writes, "namely, that my interest in boys was a lingering effect of the sex play in which I'd engaged regularly for several months with a junior high school classmate." Bawer will probably think me prurient for wishing he had given a more specific and detailed account of this experience. I mean less what he did with which parts of his body than what he was thinking and how he felt. He says he abandoned the theory when he read in his father's medical books that "sex play between adolescent boys was extremely common." That may be so, but for gay boys these episodes are almost always intensely exciting and indelible. What is one to make of Bawer's frustratingly brief, almost dismissive allusion to his first homosexual experience? One possibility is that in his case it was not in fact especially exciting. Perhaps his libido is rather anemic, which would explain why he finds the sexual raptures of the gay subculture so perverse, even incomprehensible. Or one might imagine that the experience was indeed powerful but that it triggered a repressive reaction, leading him to deny its significance at the time and distorting the memory of it since. In either case, the event that usually marks a watershed in gay autobiographies counts for very little here.

Bawer did not consciously recognize he was homosexual until he turned twenty. He attributes his slowness to his "utter lack of self-possession," by which he means, quite literally, that he did not feel he belonged to himself. He couldn't believe that his emotions, even when they were overwhelming, had any objective reality. "At the profoundest level of my subconscious," he writes, "I saw myself as belonging to my parents in mind and heart and soul." From which he concluded that if he were in fact gay, his parents would have known about it first and told him so! Bawer himself calls his reasoning "absurd." Certainly it suggests that the young Bruce Bawer was an odd psychological creature. One might wonder whether he has ever fully liberated himself from the symbiotic identification with his parents. He may have fashioned an autonomous identity as a gay man, but he remains in the shadow of their conservative worldview and values.

The moment of self-recognition at twenty was breathtakingly sudden. The feelings that had been disturbing the peace of his unconscious for years broke through, as he puts it in Kierkegaardian terms, "with the force of a thunderclap." Hugging his best friend good-bye for the Christmas holidays, he knew "instantaneously" that he was in love with the young man. The knowledge, he says, was not only abrupt but "extraordinarily joyful": "I didn't feel so much as a shadow of regret, fear, guilt, or disgust; it didn't occur to me for a moment to think that there was anything wrong or unnatural about my homosexuality. On the contrary, nothing in my life had ever felt as right and natural as this." The sudden, unmediated passage from insouciance to joy seems as improbable as his earlier belief that he couldn't be homosexual because his parents would have told him about it. He notes that his experience differed radically from that of most gay men when they first become aware of their homosexuality. But he doesn't ask why. Recalling that the epiphany must have occurred in 1976 (when Bawer became twenty), the historian is bound to think that the teachings of the Gay Liberation movement, then almost a decade old, had probably insinuated themselves into his mind in spite of himself. But of course that would imply that the ability to recognize and embrace one's identity as a homosexual is culturally contingent. Bawer, on the other hand, wants to suggest that it is a purely natural act, available to the unassisted human intelligence if it is able to respond honestly and without the artificial impediments of prejudice. Hence his insistence that he "knew instinctively," on that fateful day when he hugged his friend, that his homosexuality was natural and good, and that accepting it was "a matter of being true to myself." The account of his breakthrough as a kind of immaculate conception testifies to his unexamined essentialism and his anemic sense of history.

The real meaning of Bawer's joyful recognition of his homosexuality is not easy to assess. One cannot even be certain that it entailed a conscious admission that he wanted a physical relationship with another man. To be sure, the very word "homosexual" seems to indicate as much. But, significantly, Bawer says not that he desired his college friend but that he was in love with him. Of course one of his cardinal principles is that homosexuality is not about sex but about emotion, and he would probably accuse me of falling into the subculture's bad sexual habits for wondering about the exact erotic significance of his newfound identity. What is clear, however, is that his guiltless embrace of that identity had absolutely no consequences for either his romantic or his sexual life. Although his friend apparently reciprocated his feelings and spent hours with him almost every day for the next two years, nothing was said and certainly nothing was done. "Once in a long while," he writes, "our eyes would meet and our hands would touch, and there would be no question as to what was in our minds and hearts; yet neither of us could bring himself to speak so much as a word about what we felt." In order to resist their attraction, both men threw themselves into short-lived relationships with women. In retrospect Bawer denounces their behavior as "shameful" and "cowardly." But he doesn't explain why, if he felt his homosexuality was so "right and natural," he remained unable to express it.

We don't learn in *A Place at the Table* when he became a homosexual in practice. But the book reveals that he kept his sexual identity secret for over a decade after the moment of recognition in 1976. Indeed, as a professional journalist he remained closeted into the

1990s. At the *American Spectator*, where he wrote for much of the '80s, he told no one he was gay, though, he insists, he never said anything to imply he wasn't. He resolved to tell the truth if asked, but no one did. When the *Spectator* published homophobic pieces, such as Michael Fumento's "The Myth of Heterosexual AIDS" or P. J. O'Rourke's "Manhattan Swish" (which compares the homosexual's demand for antidiscrimination laws to a drunk's demand for free booze), Bawer justified his continued association with the magazine on the ground that if he was allowed to write what he wanted he could hardly complain that others were given the same freedom. "What's more," he adds, "I felt that as an *American Spectator* writer I had a singular opportunity to nudge its readers . . . toward a more reflective, tolerant variety of Toryism—a variety that, among other things, didn't look upon homosexuality as something to be automatically condemned or ridiculed." In 1990 he put his campaign for tolerance to work by writing sympathetically about the AIDS film *Longtime Companion* (which moved him deeply, he says, because it was the first convincing portrayal he had seen of "the everyday life of middle-class gay male couples.") When his editor refused to run his "completely innocuous" remarks, the futility of his enterprise became apparent and he resigned. Indeed, the brouhaha over *Longtime Companion* marked the turning point that led him finally to abandon the closet and write *A Place at the Table*, which is as much an attack on conservative homophobes as on gay radicals and in which the closet itself is identified as the main enabler of antigay sentiment. But for nearly a decade and a half the man who joyfully embraced his homosexual identity at twenty managed not only to keep it under wraps but to endure the professional company of bigots.

Bawer, as we've seen, insists that the moment in which he recognized his sexual identity was one of unambiguous self-affirmation. He knew immediately that his feelings were good and natural, indeed, that they were "inextricably linked to the most true and good and beautiful emotions that I'd ever experienced." Yet he is haunted by the fear that other gay boys are being deprived of this joyous experience of self-discovery by the depredations of the counterculture.

He begins his book with an anecdote meant to illustrate the problem. One day he went into a midtown Manhattan bookstore and found a teenager furtively looking at a copy of a gay weekly called the *New York Native*. Not unreasonably, he concluded that the boy was gay and proceeded to develop an elaborate fantasy about what must be going through his mind. The boy, Bawer became convinced, was a younger version of himself. "When I looked at him," he writes, "I felt as though I were seeing myself a few years earlier—confused, scared, reaching out tentatively for something that would explain to me who I was." He "knew immediately" that the teenager was just beginning to recognize his homosexuality and that he had no one—"no parent, sibling, teacher, friend, minister"—to whom he could turn for help.

And what did this young innocent find in the pages of the *New York Native*? The hideous misrepresentation of homosexuality propagated by the subculture, a lethal brew of effeminacy, sadomasochism, and promiscuity: "What leapt out at me, and stayed in my mind for some time afterwards, was . . . a photograph, probably accompanying a review of some cabaret act, of a man in drag; photographs of black-clad men in bondage, presumably in advertisements for leather bars and S&M equipment; and photographs of hunky bare-chested young men, no doubt promoting 'massages' and 'escort services' and X-rated videotapes." Bawer was so appalled by what he assumed the boy must be thinking that he felt tempted to tap him on the shoulder and deliver a lecture. Indeed, he composed the speech in his mind: " 'Don't let this magazine disturb you,' " he imagined himself saying, " 'Don't let it make you think, *Well, if that's what it means to be gay, then I guess I must not be gay.* Don't let it make you think, *Well, I'm gay, so I guess I'd better try to become like that.* And don't let it make you think, *Well, I'm gay, but I refuse to become like that, so I guess the only alternative is to repress it and marry.*' " He ends his anecdote by saying that he has written his book precisely for this boy. It is his imaginary speech writ large.

The story—which Bawer repeated in a lecture in Denver's Saint John's Episcopal Cathedral a year later—is revealing. In particular, it reveals his sublime (not to say arrogant) conviction that he knew exactly what this young man wanted and feared. But why shouldn't we imagine that the boy was drawn precisely to the erotic possibilities suggested by the photos in the *Native*? Perhaps the boy felt confined and ill-at-ease in his conventional masculinity and found the picture of a man in drag intriguing. Perhaps the thought of bondage excited him. Perhaps (most likely of all) he wished he could have sex with the "hunky bare-chested young men." After all, he might have picked up a magazine like the *Advocate* with more white-bread pictures of gay men. Yet he chose to contemplate the provocative images in the *Native*. Bawer has construed his young man—as he has construed "the silent majority" of gay men—after his own image.

At the same time I would suggest that this teenage boy also represents an object of desire for Bawer. The book makes such a heroic effort to discredit desire that one is surprised to find it insinuating itself, as it were, between the lines. "Lean and handsome [and] rather more shy and sweet-natured than the average New York City teenager," the boy in the bookstore is simply the most important installment of an erotic type that lights up the otherwise sexually antiseptic pages of *A Place at the Table*. The boys who excite Bawer are invariably tall, thin, shy, and sexually innocent. They are, in a sense, narcissistic love objects, as Bawer himself was just such a boy. So was the boy Paul—"tall, skinny, and bespectacled"—whom he fell in love with in eighth grade. Bawer spots another incarnation of the type with his parents at a Pride parade, a "tall, gangly, shy-looking" thirteen-year-old who he imagines will wake up in four or five years to the realization that he is gay. All are examples of what he elsewhere refers to as "a certain fresh-scrubbed, middle-American winsomeness." "There are few things as fascinating," he allows, "as the psychology of a gay person who doesn't yet know that he is gay." Perhaps significantly, he imagines that had he in fact spoken to the young reader of the *New York Native*, the boy would have thought he was making a pass and raced away, "his heart pounding."

I offer this speculation not as a reproach to Bawer. On the contrary, I find him more human and attractive for betraying that he is turned on by a certain kind of looks and demeanor. It makes for an agreeable contrast with his ponderous announcement, shortly after the bookstore boy has put in his appearance, "I'm a monogamous, churchgoing Christian." Bawer of course might well admit to the attraction and say that the important thing is that he didn't succumb to it. For the sake of morality and the well-being of our primary relationship, such temptations must be resisted, whereas the subculture not only fails to resist but actively encourages us to indulge. If the spark of desire I have discovered in Bawer's pages is genuine, it means that his austerity is not just the product of a less than exigent libido (as one is sometimes tempted to think) but the willful imposition of a deeply held sexual philosophy on his sometimes recalcitrant desires. This is, I admit, a fearsome prospect to contemplate for anyone who considers himself a friend of pleasure. But it makes Bawer a more interesting and potent moralist, with something of the intellectual gravitas of the great theological adepts of denial like Saint Paul or Saint Augustine.

Critics of gay conservatives like Richard Goldstein have observed that Bawer's *A Place at the Table* has enjoyed nothing like the influence of Andrew Sullivan's *Virtually Normal*, published just two years later, even though the books espouse very similar points of view. Perhaps Sullivan's book got more attention because its author was the prominent young editor of the *New Republic* and thus a more visible public intellectual. *Virtually Normal* is also a more systematic work of political polemic, with greater intellectual pretensions (as when it takes on Michel Foucault, who goes unmentioned in *A Place at the Table*). Bawer's manner is casual and anecdotal; he moves from topic to topic according to no discernible pattern. But I find him a more engaging writer than Sullivan, even as he embraces views with which I disagree or find downright repugnant. His manifest sincerity, his cheerful willingness to say unpopular things, and his genuine skill as a storyteller make him an effective advocate for his cause—and make *A Place at the Table* the central expression of the new gay conservatism.

CHAPTER TWO

Andrew Sullivan and His Enemies

Andrew Sullivan has written extensively about homosexuality over the past decade and a half. Without question the most important of these writings is his book *Virtually Normal: An Argument about Homosexuality* (1995), which offers a systematic analysis of the different ways of thinking about homosexuality and the political order. In 1998 he published a second book, *Love Undetectable: Notes on Friendship, Sex, and Survival*, a collection of three long essays on AIDS, the causes of homosexuality, and the place of friendship in gay life. In addition, he has written dozens of articles on topics ranging from gay marriage to testosterone in journals like the *New Republic*, the *New York Times Magazine*, and the *Advocate*. Most recently he has taken to producing a web log (or "blog"), www.andrewsullivan.com, in which he gives his views on the events of the day. By mid-2003 it had become the most successful web log on the Internet, with more than 1.5 million visits a month. During the past year he has been obsessed with promoting the U.S. war against Iraq, but he also uses the blog to advance his ideas about current matters affecting gays such as the pedophilia scandal in the Roman Catholic Church. Taken together it is a substantial body of work, and it has made Sullivan the most influential gay public intellectual in the country. Indeed, his critics, like Richard Goldstein, complain bitterly about the authority Sullivan has garnered as a spokesman for gay issues. He is certainly the best known of the figures treated in this book.

Virtually Normal is an elaboration of the ideas Sullivan presented in a 1993 article in the *New Republic*, "The Politics of Homosexuality." Michael Warner, who is perhaps Sullivan's fiercest opponent, calls it "the most influential gay essay of the nineties." I want to begin with a consideration of the analytic categories that *Virtually Normal* deploys to map the range of interpretations to which homosexuality has been subjected. The fashioning of these categories represents Sullivan's most obvious attempt to establish his credentials as an important thinker, indeed, as a kind of philosopher of homosexuality. Where Bruce Bawer is satisfied to present his views in a casual, even anecdotal fashion, Sullivan aspires to treat the subject with systematic rigor. The intellectual ambitions of *Virtually Normal* reflect Sullivan's professional training in political philosophy: he earned a Ph.D. at Harvard, writing a dissertation on the political theorist Michael Oakeshott under the direction of Harvey Mansfield. He may make his living as a journalist, but he clearly wants to be taken seriously as an intellectual.

Sullivan proposes that thinking about homosexuality and politics can be divided into four schools, which (proceeding from right to left) he calls the prohibitionists, the conservatives, the liberals, and the liberationists. He acknowledges the artificiality of these categories but insists, reasonably, on their heuristic usefulness. The prohibitionists are religious believers—both Roman Catholic and fundamentalist Protestant—for whom homosexual acts are morally evil and the individuals who commit them, sinfully responsible for their erotic misdeeds. In other words, the prohibitionists make no distinction between homosexual behavior and homosexual orientation, which in effect doesn't exist for them. The conservatives, by contrast, accept that a small portion of the population is involuntarily inclined to homosexuality but believe that homosexual behavior is nonetheless undesirable and should be discouraged for the health of society. Their view might be characterized as Burkean: they hold that the state acts properly when it discourages behavior not conducive to social well-being.

On the other side of the argument stand the liberals and the liberationists, both of whom are defenders of homosexuality and critics of discrimination. By liberalism Sullivan understands the modern American variety of the species, which wishes to use state intervention to promote social justice. In the case of homosexuality, liberalism advocates antidiscrimination laws, which it hopes will control the behavior and ultimately overcome the prejudices of homophobes, just as they are used to combat racism and sexism. Finally, by liberationists Sullivan means, above all, queer theorists (headed, in his view, by Michel Foucault), who regard the category of homosexuality as itself a new form of oppression and embrace a politics that would free human sexuality from the fixed identities (homosexual, heterosexual, bisexual) into which it has been packaged. The liberationists, in this analysis, are in secret intellectual alliance with the prohibitionists, because, even though they stand for opposite views of sexual morality and utterly loathe one another, they agree that homosexual identity (in contrast to homosexual behavior) doesn't properly exist. Sullivan says nothing about the relative size or influence of these four groups of controversialists. He merely insists that they represent distinctive polemical traditions, each of which, in his view, is wrong. Accordingly, his analysis of these traditions is followed by a final chapter in which he gives his own prescription for a satisfactory politics of homosexuality, one that avoids the pitfalls of the older schools of thought.

The most striking feature of Sullivan's treatment of the prohibitionists (and to a lesser extent of the conservatives) is the attitude of respect he brings to their arguments. In general, contemporary gays regard these arguments as little more than intellectually dressed-up bigotry. They are not to be debated but dismissed out of hand or shouted down. Sullivan, however, is writing his book, at least in part, to convince his ideological friends on the right to amend their views of homosexuality, which means that he must address the arguments on which conservatives have relied to justify their hostility. Therefore he begins by asserting that prohibitionism boasts a worthy intellectual pedigree, one whose claims must be carefully evaluated. "As arguments go," he writes, "it has a rich literature, an extensive history, a complex philosophical core, and a view of humanity that tells a coherent and at times beautiful story of the meaning of our natural selves." To be sure, the arguments have sometimes been used to "prettify" prejudice, but they nonetheless deserve to be taken seriously.

The centerpiece of the prohibitionist argument is the notion that homosexuality is a choice, which means that there is no significant difference between homosexual acts and homosexual orientation. "Being" a homosexual consists of a willingness to commit those acts and a history of doing so. Homosexuality, in other words, is not a deep and abiding identity but a relatively superficial and contingent phenomenon, "such as a propensity to lie or a fondness for wasting money." The proper moral attitude toward homosexuality is to demand that the individual stop committing the acts, which is, in effect, to stop being a homosexual.

Sullivan examines three main sources of prohibitionist opinion: the Bible, natural law theory, and the recent pronouncements of the Roman Catholic Church, notably Cardinal Joseph Ratzinger's 1986 address, "On the Pastoral Care of Homosexual Persons." Sullivan subjects all three to a kind of casuistic analysis in which he identifies contradictions and unanticipated consequences that undermine the force of the argument for prohibition. Here as elsewhere one is conscious of the erstwhile Oxford debater, who is fond of tying his opponents in logical knots and exposing their conceptual failings. The sweet talk about a "rich," "extensive," "complex" tradition that tells a "coherent" and "beautiful" story gives way to a brutal exposition of intellectual malfeasance. One is left wondering if his original expression of admiration wasn't disingenuous—a ploy to puff up an opponent he is about to lay low.

Like Bruce Bawer, Sullivan relies almost entirely on John Boswell's *Christianity, Social Tolerance, and Homosexuality: Gay People in Western Europe from the Beginning of the Christian Era to the Fourteenth Century* to dispose of the biblical objections to homosexuality. Because he assumes that a significant number of his readers are believing Christians and Jews, he can't simply dismiss these antique religious opinions as so much errant nonsense. Instead, he embraces Boswell's labored demonstrations that the notorious passages from Leviticus and Saint Paul don't really mean what they appear to mean—that, properly interpreted, the Bible is not homophobic. At the same time, he distances himself a bit from this apologetic enterprise by observing, "There is something a little desperate about those who argue that the Bible has no view about homosexual acts."

He next considers Saint Thomas Aquinas's "peerless and majestic articulation" of natural law theory. The theory holds that all human beings have a single basic nature and purpose, which can be ascertained, essentially, from observation. An examination of nature, Aquinas argues, reveals that the purpose of sex is procreation, from which it follows that sexual acts that do not result, at least potentially, in procreation are unnatural. Homosexuality spectacularly fails the procreation test and therefore stands condemned.

The trouble with this argument, according to Sullivan, is that while it claims to base itself on the evidence of nature, it doesn't give an adequate account of what nature actually reveals about sexual behavior. In particular, it ignores the empirical evidence that homosexuality has been a constant reality throughout natural history. Thus a truly complete account of sexual behavior would have to include the observation that in some cases—the exact percentage is unimportant—members of the same sex engage in sexual acts.

The contradiction is not perhaps as telling as Sullivan thinks. Aquinas doesn't deny that same-sex acts occur in nature. How could he, when the purpose of his analysis is to explain why such acts should be condemned? Sullivan must show that Aquinas overlooks not just the natural evidence of homosexual behavior but the natural evidence of homosexual orientation. And while he can say accurately that scientists and historians agree about the universality of homosexual acts, he knows that there is no such agreement about homosexual orientation. On the contrary, a good deal of historical scholarship in the last quarter century has argued that homosexual orientation is a relatively isolated modern phenomenon. Sullivan of course disagrees with that scholarship, but its existence means he can't argue that Aquinas's reasoning has been confounded by the consensus of scientists and scholars.

A second difficulty with the natural law theory of homosexuality is posed by the existence of sterile heterosexuals. Sullivan gives a cheeky version of this objection in a *New Republic* article of 1996 subtitled "Why Does Pat Buchanan Have No Kids?" If procreation—or at least the possibility of procreation—is the sole criterion for deciding whether sexual acts are legitimate, then, Sullivan says, sexual relations between infertile straights should be subject to the same strictures as homosexuality. Because Pat Buchanan—America's leading Roman Catholic homophobe—has been married for many years but has no children, Sullivan infers, "Either Buchanan is using contraception, in which case he is a hypocrite; or he or his wife is infertile, and he is, one assumes, engaging in nonprocreative sex. Either way, I can see no good reason why his sexual life is any more sinful than mine." Although the argument overlooks some darker possibilities— that the Buchanans have no sex life, that Buchanan is impotent, that he is homosexual—it makes an effective debater's point. It does not, however, address what might be called the argument from "symbolic complementarity," which points to the seemingly natural fit of male and female genitals as the ultimate basis for privileging heterosexual intercourse. "Even with sterile people," Sullivan concedes, "there is a symbolism in the union of male and female that speaks to the core nature of sexual congress and to its virtuous instantiation." He counters, rather weakly, that the symbolic argument speaks only to the *centrality* of heterosexual intercourse in nature, not to its exclusiveness. The argument probably needs to be taken more seriously. I suspect it provides the deepest intellectual anchor for the conviction that homosexuality is unnatural.

Sullivan's treatment of Cardinal Ratzinger again begins with a show of respect. It makes for a striking contrast with Paul Monette's portrait of the same figure in his autobiography, *Becoming a Man*, where we read: "A new Inquisition is in full cry, led by the rabid dog in brocade, Cardinal Ratzinger of the Curia, the malevolent divine who laid down the law that loving gay was a matter of 'intrinsic evil.' " Sullivan's analysis focuses on the contradictions that arise when Ratzinger at once revises the Church's traditional denial of homosexual orientation and hardens its opposition to homosexual behavior. By admitting that homosexual persons truly exist and should be the object of the Church's pastoral care, Ratzinger moves Roman Catholicism away from its long-standing prohibitionist view of homosexuality. But in the very same document he perversely ratchets up the Church's categorical condemnation of homosexual acts. "The document," Sullivan concludes, "is asking us . . . to love the sinner more deeply than ever before, but to hate the sin even more passionately." As a practicing Roman Catholic, Sullivan is deeply distressed by his church's heartlessly contradictory views, and, although he remains faithful, one gets the impression that he has been stretched to the breaking point. When the Vatican seemed prepared to use the recent pedophilia scandal as an excuse to kick all homosexuals out of the priesthood, he announced on his web log that he has stopped going to mass and now feels that those who say Roman Catholicism and gayness are incompatible may be right.

To this reader, Sullivan's second category of theorists, the conservatives, are the most odious of his four groups of controversialists. Unlike Saint Paul, Saint Thomas Aquinas, or even Cardinal Ratzinger, they are sophisticated modern intellectuals who cannot be excused for spouting hateful nonsense on the grounds of benighted antiquity. But Sullivan treats their arguments with the same patient respect he lavished on the prohibitionists. He calls them "brave, . . . honest, and intelligent." Where the prohibitionists are concerned with moral absolutes, the conservatives justify their views by appealing to the stability and flourishing of society. They concede that "some small minority" of individuals is involuntarily homosexual, and they recognize that to persecute such individuals is unjust. But they believe no less strongly that homosexual behavior is socially harmful and should be discouraged. They take a benign view of the closet, because the most sensible way to treat homosexuality, in their opinion, is with respectful silence. As Sullivan puts it, "They are tolerant of private homosexuals and disapproving of public ones."

Sullivan examines the arguments of two conservative theorists: the Oxford natural law scholar John Finnis and the Harvard psychologist E. L. Pattullo. At the heart of John Finnis's "intelligible and subtle account of homosexuality" is the conviction that homosexual relations, if publicly affirmed, pose a threat to heterosexual marriage. The reasoning by which Finnis arrives at this conclusion is unusually tortured (and advanced in no less tortured prose). The basic idea is that same-sex sexual relations send a dangerous message: they suggest that the purpose of sex is individual gratification rather than the emotional and physical binding of a procreative couple. Because the stability of the procreative couple is vital to the well-being of society, all public messages that subvert the channeling of sexual desire into exclusively marital, heterosexual, and loving relationships should be censored. Homosexuality, in other words, threatens the way straight couples need to understand the role of sex in their lives and its social implications: "The deliberate genital coupling of persons of the same sex is repudiated [because] . . . it treats human sexual capacities in a way which is deeply hostile to the self-understanding of those members of the community who are willing to commit themselves to real marriage in the understanding that its sexual joys are not mere instruments to, or mere compensations for, the accomplishment of marriage's responsibilities, but rather enable the spouses to *actualize and experience* their intelligent commitment to share in those responsibilities, in that genuine self-giving." Society thus acts prudently when it asserts that homosexual behavior is "shameful, delusional, self-destructive, and corrosive."

E. L. Pattullo's analysis of the homosexual problem is almost identical to Finnis's—homosexuals should not be persecuted but homosexual behavior should be publicly discouraged—though the focus is slightly different. Pattullo is less concerned with shoring up hetero-sexual marriage than with cutting down on the number of individuals who decide to pursue a homosexual life. That is, although he admits that most homosexuals come to their identity involuntarily, he also believes there are a number of individuals who could be dissuaded from going the homosexual route if they got the right message at the right time. He calls these individuals "waverers." If society proclaims that homosexual relations are as valid as heterosexual relations (as proponents of gay rights would have it), these waverers will have no incentive to choose the heterosexual option. "Reason suggests," con-cludes Pattullo, "that we guard against doing anything which might mislead wavering children into perceiving society as indifferent to the sexual orientation they might develop."

Bruce Bawer also discusses Pattullo's argument in *A Place at the Table*. He finds much object to in it, not least that it justifies treating homosexuals as second-class citizens on the grounds that such treat-ment might have a desirable effect on the undecided. More important, Bawer simply denies that there are genuine "waverers," persons who would embrace heterosexuality if they got the right message. "When [Pattullo] speaks of 'waverers' he is speaking of homosexuals who refuse to accept their homosexuality." Sullivan, by contrast, empha-sizes the implausibility of the fear—in both Finnis and Pattullo—that a more tolerant attitude toward homosexuality would endanger the health of heterosexual marriage and thus the well-being of society. In particular, he disputes the notion that public acceptance of ho-mosexuality would undermine the "self-understanding" of the het-erosexual family. Homosexuals, he points out, are themselves mem-bers of families—the sons and daughters, brothers and sisters, even fathers and mothers of heterosexuals. To treat them with contempt does not shore up the traditional family but in fact corrodes it: "Ho-mosexual sons and daughters who are denied the love and support of their families are liable to turn against the institution of the family, to wound and destroy it, out of hurt and rejection. And parents, incul-cated in the kind of disdain of homosexuality conservatives claim is necessary to protect the family, react to the existence of gay children with unconscionable anger and pain, and actually help destroy loving families."

The conservatives also fail to acknowledge the contribution homosexuals make to the upbringing and shaping of future generations. Gays may not create and raise children (although of course increasing numbers of them do that as well), but they play a disproportionate role in the institutions that complete the family's task: "Homosexuals have often turned their literal inability to have children into an extraordinary desire to beget figurative children: in the teaching professions, the arts, the military, political and intellectual life." They compensate for what they don't contribute to the genetic family through their labors on behalf of "the social family at large."

In the end, Sullivan insists, there is no contradiction between promoting the traditional family and promoting "stable" homosexual relationships. He even argues that the existence of enduring homosexual relationships serves to buttress the institution of heterosexual marriage, for the simple reason that such relationships are clearly modeled after heterosexual unions. That is precisely why radicals dislike gay marriage: it harnesses homosexuality to a deeply traditional institution. "Why," he asks, "should conservatives oppose it?"

II

Sullivan's treatment of the liberal conception of homosexuality differs from his treatment of the other three schools of opinion in that he mentions no individual theorists. Indeed, liberalism in his analysis is less an intellectual than a political tradition. It is, in fact, the politics embraced by the mainstream gay organizations in the United States, groups like the Human Rights Campaign or the National Gay and Lesbian Task Force. To speak more precisely, it is one particular plank in their platform, namely, the effort to pass antidiscrimination and hate crime legislation for gays analogous to that for women and minorities.

As a classical liberal—a disciple, as he makes clear, of John Stuart Mill—Sullivan takes a dim view of these laws, not just for gays but

for women and minorities as well. He objects to their illiberal consequences: in the interests of promoting a social good—tolerance and
equality—they violate the freedom of the individual, in particular,
freedom of contract (as when they force the individual to rent a room
or give a job against his will) and freedom of expression (as when they
outlaw the public use of particular words). He grudgingly admits that
in the case of blacks the sacrifice of individual freedom is justified,
because the force of racist prejudice is such as to render the formal
guarantees of liberty and equality (as in the Fourteenth Amendment)
meaningless. But the situation of gays is different. Here the evil of cur-
tailing individual liberty is not outweighed by any good that antidiscrimination and hate crime legislation might achieve. "The trade-off
which seemed defensible with regard to race seems far less defensible," he writes, "in the case of sexual orientation."

Sullivan of course doesn't deny that gays suffer discrimination that
is sometimes as violent and damaging as that suffered by blacks. On
the contrary, he argues that antigay prejudice can do even more harm
than racism: "If the stigma is attached not simply to an obviously random characteristic, such as skin pigmentation, but to the deepest desires of the human heart, then it can eat away at a person's sense of
his or her own dignity with peculiar ferocity." He notes further that
young gays confront homophobic prejudice entirely alone, whereas
young blacks enjoy the support of family and friends when they must
deal with racism for the first time. He also thinks that homophobia
is uniquely painful because "it attacks the very heart of what makes a
human being human: the ability to love and be loved."

Still, he insists that the circumstance of gays is ultimately less dire
than that of blacks. In his view the essential difference between sexual
orientation and race is visibility: "Race is always visible; sexuality can
be hidden." Unlike blacks, gays can pass. This simple fact "accords
them a degree of choice in their predicament that more obviously
identifiable racial types cannot enjoy." Another way of making the
same point is to say that there is less agreement about how to define
homosexuality than about how to define race. Some think homosexuality is a form of behavior, while others think it is an identity. Most

definitions combine both behavior and identity. Although gender and race also have a behavioral component, they are "more clearly identifiable as identities." Because of the ambiguity about who is a homosexual and because gays can pass, antigay prejudice is less inexorable than racial prejudice.

Sullivan seems unaware that a good deal of recent thinking about race challenges his flat assertion that race is visible. Critical race theorists argue that race is socially constructed—that it is more cultural than biological. But I think Sullivan's point can survive this challenge. His argument depends less on the fact of racial visibility than on the social conviction that it is visible. The vast majority of Americans believe that blackness can be seen while gayness—save in the case of the hopelessly flaming—cannot. That is the difference one needs to bear in mind in assessing the relative difficulty faced by a young person coming into an awareness of his racial or sexual identity. The gay boy or girl always has the option of the closet, an institution that has no racial counterpart.

One might agree with Sullivan that the case for antidiscrimination laws to protect gays is less exigent than the case for blacks yet still argue that such laws are needed, especially in a world where the closet is no longer considered a legitimate option. But against any benefits the laws might bring Sullivan weighs the profound antipathy, even bitterness, they inspire in the substantial part of the population with deep religious objections to homosexuality. "For many people in Western societies," he writes, "the sexual and emotional entanglement of two people of the same gender is a moral enormity." In a free society these people may be willing to leave homosexuals alone, but they can't bear being told that they must put up with their company on the job or rent housing to them: "Anti-discrimination statutes that force them to do so are an affront to these people, and a flagrant violation, from their point of view, of the moral neutrality of the liberal state." For Sullivan, the fact that so many people are affronted—and their homophobia intensified—by these laws is sufficient grounds to forgo them.

Sullivan doesn't always show such concern for the sensibilities of homophobes. In the case of the military's antigay policy, for example, he is contemptuous of the argument that out gays should be barred from serving because their presence would disturb straights and thus undermine morale. In this instance his view seems to be that public policy should not be determined by anything so trivial as mere offense. But surely the main shortcoming in his analysis of antidiscrimination laws is his failure to acknowledge that they are largely symbolic. He notes that where such laws have been passed, they are almost never used. That is because in reality they are an exercise in consciousness-raising: they represent an authoritative statement against discrimination that aims to make its victims feel included while its authors are shamed. Of course, Sullivan could point out that the laws have not had the desired psychological effect: they may make gays feel better, but they seem only to have intensified the aversion of homophobes. He may well be right when he concludes that "the subject of homosexuality, like the subject of abortion, is simply too deep, too emotional, too visceral to be resolved by the calm voice of liberal legalism."

*   *   *

I am doing a certain violence to Sullivan's analysis in *Virtually Normal* by taking up his treatment of the "liberationist" tradition last. He himself places it in second position, right after prohibitionism. The juxtaposition is strategic: he intends to draw attention to an important affinity between the most conservative and the most radical ways of thinking about homosexuality. As he puts it, the two traditions exhibit "a perfect symmetry." Liberationism is "a kind of reverse image" of prohibitionism, "locked in doctrinal combat with its arguments and theses." In effect, he embraces Bruce Bawer's notion that radicals and reactionaries on the homosexual issue represent mirror images of one another.

What unites liberationists and prohibitionists conceptually is their common rejection of the idea of homosexual identity or orientation. In the case of the liberationists this rejection takes the form of the doctrine that the homosexual is "a construct of human thought" rather than "an inherent or natural state of being." In nature, as it were, there are just homosexual acts. Only under certain historical conditions is the bearer of those acts understood—or "constructed"—as a homosexual person, meaning someone whose deepest and most enduring identity is defined by attraction to the same sex. Furthermore, the liberationists consider this construction largely regrettable: it entails a reduction of the individual's erotic potential to a single, limited capacity, when in fact we long for a fluid and polymorphous sexuality. "For the liberationists," Sullivan writes, "the full end of human fruition is to be free of all social constructs, to be liberated from the condition of homosexuality into a fully chosen form of identity, which is a repository of individual acts of freedom."

Sullivan identifies Michel Foucault as the preeminent author of this way of thinking about homosexuality. Foucault, he says, plays the same role for liberationism as Thomas Aquinas plays for prohibitionism. Accordingly, much of Sullivan's chapter on liberationism is given over to a discussion of Foucault's thought. He obviously hopes to establish his credentials as an intellectual heavyweight by taking on this iconic and difficult postmodern thinker. And while he does a reasonable job of expounding Foucault's ideas, he fails to make a case for their influence on gay activists. The truth is that Foucault has found a home almost entirely in the academy. There is, as a result, a certain feeling of inconsequence about Sullivan's elaborate engagement with Foucault. One can't escape feeling that his treatment is more a matter of intellectual display than a genuine attempt to understand the thinking of the gay left.

Sullivan takes issue with the radical constructionism at the heart of the liberationist position. He admits that the way homosexuality is understood and experienced varies greatly from one culture or one era to the next. He mentions David Greenberg's *The Construction of Homosexuality* and George Chauncey's *Gay New York: Gender, Urban Culture, and the Makings of the Gay Male World, 1890–1940* as showing how differently same-sex behavior has been interpreted over time and space. But in the end Sullivan insists that beneath all the historical and cultural variations there remains a certain common experience of the homosexual condition. His position is at bottom a humanist one: some element of real individuality always escapes the social system, no matter how oppressive. "Human beings," he writes, "are not social constructions all the way down. They have a will and a personality that is understandable across cultures and across time and that constitutes the material on which constructions can be built."

Sullivan defends this essentialist view of homosexual identity above all by appealing to his own experience. Sometimes, to be sure, he argues that the historical record of all societies provides evidence not just of homosexual behavior but of "distinct homosexual identities and communities and subcultures." He knows, however, that many scholars have challenged this view, and he clearly feels more comfortable relying on his personal sense of homosexual desire as something so profound, enduring, and inescapable that he can safely conclude it transcends history and culture. His experience convinces him that that in all societies and at all times somewhere between 2 and 5 percent of the population feels an involuntary attraction to their own sex. He thus confidently rejects that Foucauldian theory that the homosexual is a modern invention.

The argument might seem to imply that, like most gay conservatives, Sullivan holds to a simple essentialist conception of homosexuality. But in fact his view of this issue is more nuanced. Even as he contends that some basic human reality escapes all social constructions, his ideas about the causes of homosexuality—which he presents in the second essay of *Love Undetectable*, "Virtually Abnormal"— commit him to a fairly soft variety of essentialism. In the essay he expresses a strong preference for Freud's theory of the origins of homosexuality—which sees the condition resulting from a complex interplay of biological and experiential factors—over the strict biological determinism of Richard Isay. But even Freud's theory has an essentialist feel about it in that it views homosexual orientation as determined by early childhood experiences over which the individual has no more control than over his genetic predisposition. Sullivan's enthusiasm for Freud is, in my reading, unique among gay conservatives. "For all of Freud's obvious failings," he writes, "I defy any honest homosexual to read Freud's work in this area and not find something worth pondering about his own development or the associations of his own desires." In particular, the Freudian etiology that locates the origin of male homosexuality in the child's excessive attachment to the mother and alienation from the father—an etiology that has often been criticized as homophobic—wins Sullivan's approval, although he is inclined to think that the alienation from the father is more likely a result than a cause of homosexuality.

Sullivan's effort to link liberationist thinking to radical politics is entirely unpersuasive. He says that three political phenomena of the 1980s and early 1990s were products of doctrinaire social constructionism: outing, the policing of language, and ACT UP. Outing is the practice, associated with the journalist Michelangelo Signorile, of exposing prominent closeted homosexuals as a way of attacking the institution of the closet. Sullivan admits that he can point to no direct intellectual influence of Foucault on the proponents of outing, but he nonetheless insists that it has a Foucauldian logic: "This tactic sees the nexus of power inherent in the 'privacy' that society gives to homosexuals and seeks to resist it at its nerve center, exercising in perfect Foucauldian fashion a form of rebellion against a discourse of power designed to oppress the queer." The language is sufficiently opaque to make Sullivan sound like a queer theorist himself, but it can't disguise the blatant illogic of his case. After all, outing is based on the assumption that homosexual identity is entirely real. The philosopher K. Anthony Appiah draws attention to this contradiction in a review of *Virtually Normal* in the *New York Review of Books*: "How can someone who asserts that homosexuality 'does not properly exist,' as Foucault is alleged to have done, be the intellectual ancestor of a practice that presupposes that 'homosexual' is what the outed person 'really' is?"

The particular manifestation of language policing Sullivan has in mind is the insistence on "queer" rather than "gay" as the label of choice. He is right that "queer" is favored by radicals and that it often implies a constructionist point of view. But Sullivan's precise complaint is that those who insist on "queer" are guilty of imposing "a single and particular identity" on all homosexuals, rather like the "gay sensibility" that Bruce Bawer regrets. To the extent that gay radicals harbor such totalitarian aspirations (and Sullivan's characterization seems wildly overstated to me), they can hardly do so in the name of Michel Foucault, who rejects all such labels as vehicles of disciplinary oppression. There is more than a whiff of essentialism in the demand that everyone call himself queer.

Sullivan has mixed feelings about ACT UP. He regrets its divisiveness (and its absence from the battles over the military and gay marriage), but he admires its "brilliant tactical victories" against the government's drug policies. He pronounces ACT UP Foucauldian on the grounds that it treats politics as a form of theater, mistaking "the methods of art" for the "methods of persuasion." It is no accident, he says, that the founder of ACT UP, Larry Kramer, is a playwright. Whatever merit one might find in this derivation, it conveniently overlooks the fact that ACT UP protesters were much more likely to be old-fashioned essentialists than social constructionists. Larry Kramer himself has denounced constructionism as a piece of reactionary academic nonsense. Moreover, Kramer is representative not just of ACT UP but of the whole tradition of gay radicalism from Stonewall to the present. Social constructionism has been largely a scholarly addiction, while the vast majority of those who have fought in the trenches have entertained a conception of homosexual identity not that different from Sullivan's own.

Having failed to pin outing, language policing, and ACT UP on Foucault, Sullivan makes one final effort to blame gay misbehavior on the intellectual excesses of the liberationists. In *Love Undetectable* he suggests that social constructionism is ultimately responsible for gay promiscuity and, hence, for AIDS. "There is little doubt," he writes, "that the ideology that human beings are mere social constructions and that sex is beyond good and evil facilitated a world in which gay men literally killed each other by the thousands." We have to picture the patrons at gay bathhouses in the 1970s managing to shed their inhibitions only with the assistance of Foucault's *History of Sexuality.* The idea is nothing short of daffy. The case that Nazism was caused by the operas of Richard Wagner is, by comparison, almost sober.

Sullivan's own solution to the political problem of homosexuality is a version of nineteenth-century liberalism. It might reasonably be called libertarian. It takes its inspiration from John Stuart Mill, particularly *On Liberty*, though it is more rigid in its adherence to laissez-faire doctrine than Mill himself. The goal of gay politics, Sullivan argues, should be to eliminate all forms of government-sponsored inequality, while leaving private individuals free to entertain their prejudices and even put them into practice: "This politics affirms a simple and limited principle: that all *public* (as opposed to private) discrimination against homosexuals be ended and that every right and responsibility that heterosexuals enjoy as public citizens be extended to those who grow up and find themselves emotionally different. *And that is all.*" An end to public discrimination means abolishing sodomy law; guaranteeing recourse to the courts if gays do not receive equal protection from the police and equal treatment from government agencies; teaching the facts about homosexuality in government-funded schools ("although almost certainly with far less emphasis, because of homosexuality's relative rareness when compared with heterosexuality"); opening the military to out gays; and, most important, legalizing gay marriage. What should be abandoned is any effort to use the law to impose tolerance on private citizens. Here of course Sullivan is thinking of antidiscrimination and hate crime legislation—those offensive and ineffectual remedies advocated by modern, interventionist liberalism. Rather, bigots should be left their freedom, including the freedom to withhold jobs and housing from homosexuals. Only a politics of "public equality–private freedom" will move gays beyond the impasse in which they are still treated unequally by the state while they waste their political capital in a futile effort to force straights to welcome them into civil society.

The great advantage of such a politics, according to Sullivan, is that it will dramatically improve relations between gays and straights because it eliminates the irritant of imposed tolerance: "By actually disentangling from each other legally, by avoiding any actual interaction in which citizens seek legal redress from other citizens about homosexuality, this politics helps diffuse the fraught and terminal wrangling into which gay-straight relations can degenerate." No doubt homophobes will appreciate being left alone with their prejudices, but all evidence indicates they are even more angered by the effort to grant gays full legal equality than by antidiscrimination laws. The campaign for gays in the military and especially for gay marriage has unleashed a torrent of hostility that quite dwarfs the bad feelings created by the prospect of being forced to rent to gays or give them a job. Sullivan is surely right to demand legal equality, but his contention that a focus on state-sponsored discrimination will improve the atmosphere between gays and straights is manifestly mistaken.

Several critics have also complained that Sullivan's distinction between public and private is out of touch with the realities of modern life. The political theorist Alan Ryan, writing in the *New Yorker*, makes the point trenchantly: "Sullivan draws the [public-private] distinction in the traditional way: the *state* is obliged to treat all citizens alike, but private individuals may do what they choose with their own private property, may express whatever private opinions they like, and may associate with whomever they choose. Since the rise of the modern corporation, a hundred years ago, this has seemed a bit too simple. Being discriminated against by General Motors or J. P. Stevens is not quite like being sacked by one farmer when there are a dozen others to work for. And while few of us would be indignant about a family that declined to rent the spare bedroom to a Jehovah's Witness, we might feel less comfortable if the owner of a mammoth housing development made the same decision." Anthony Appiah makes the identical criticism at greater length in his *New York Review of Books* piece on *Virtually Normal*. One could argue that the history of modern American liberalism, especially since the New Deal, has been a prolonged effort to come to terms with the realities of corporate capitalism and to recognize that the classic laissez-faire nostrums no longer suffice. Sullivan either ignores that history or considers it benighted. He writes as if we were still living in the nineteenth century.

The centerpiece of Sullivan's proposed program is gay marriage. In both of his books and in numerous journal articles he has written more extensively and passionately about gay marriage than any other topic. He has even edited an anthology about it, *Same-Sex Marriage: Pro and Con*. In *Virtually Normal* he asserts, "If nothing else were done at all, and gay marriage were legalized, ninety percent of the political work necessary to achieve gay and lesbian equality would have been achieved. It is ultimately the only reform that truly matters." How he arrives at the 90 percent figure is impossible to know, but the statement makes his enormous expectations transparent.

Sullivan thinks that legalizing gay marriage would have its profoundest effect on the self-perception and psychological well-being of gay children. As gay marriage "sank into the subtle background consciousness of the culture," gay boys and girls would come into their sexual identity with the knowledge that they have a future. Where earlier generations of gay children despaired of ever finding the sort of relationship their parents enjoyed, their successors would have before their eyes (or in their cultural lexicon) evidence that they were not excluded from such a prospect. They would have access to "some older faces to apply to their unfolding lives, some language in which their identity could be properly discussed." Most important, they would no longer associate the fulfillment of their sexual needs with deviance and degradation. Rather, sex would now be linked to at least the possibility of a socially approved relationship, as it is for straights: "They would be able to feel by the intimation of a myriad examples that in this respect their emotional orientation was not merely about pleasure, or sin, or shame . . . but about the ability to love and be loved as complete, imperfect human beings." In effect, gay marriage would transform gay adolescents from self-hating sybarites into well-adjusted romantics.

Sullivan puts great emphasis on the desirable effect gay marriage would have on gay sexual behavior. He sees it is a major antidote to promiscuity, which, in his view, corrodes romantic relationships and is responsible for the AIDS epidemic. His critics, like Michael Warner, charge that his devotion to gay marriage is inspired by a deep-seated puritanism and hostility to pleasure. In reality, as we'll see, Sullivan's sexual views are interestingly ambivalent, and he can't be automatically identified with the austerity of Bruce Bawer. But unquestionably he sees the taming of male libido as one of the main benefits of gay marriage. He predicts it would increase the number of gay men who "yearn for social stability, for anchors for their relationships, for the family support and financial security that come with marriage." Where gay life is now associated with erotic adventuring, a growing number of married homosexuals would establish a new public image of the gay male, one whose sexual life is "linked to stability and love." Accordingly, he urges the advocates of gay marriage "to stress the link between gay marriage and monogamy." The resulting reformation of gay sexual manners would mean greater psychological contentment as well as protection against disease, and it would also have the happy effect of reducing homophobia, because straights would no longer perceive gay men as dangerous sexual aliens. Rather, they would come to be viewed as "virtually normal," aspiring to the same emotional and sexual goals as heterosexuals.

Sullivan's high expectations for marriage rest on his belief that it has a greater impact on human psychology than any other social institution. The right to marry, he says, is "the mark of ultimate human respect," and denying it to gays causes "the deepest psychological and political wound imaginable." Including gays within the institution of marriage, by contrast, would confer "the highest form of social approval imaginable" and is, accordingly, "the deepest means for the liberation of homosexuals." These categorical pronouncements about the psychological effects of marriage are simple articles of faith for Sullivan. They are not supported—in his texts—by evidence or even argument. He does not, for example, consider the fact that many gays claim to have achieved a perfectly satisfactory sense of well-being without the benefit of marriage, just as do the ever-increasing number of straights who choose not to marry. Marriage, most everyone agrees, is not what it once was, and Sullivan's conviction that it has unique and almost magical powers to transform consciousness seems quaintly old-fashioned. The right to marry might well make a difference in the way gays, especially young and impressionable gays, feel about themselves. But one can reasonably doubt that it would have the earth-shaking consequences Sullivan imagines.

K. Anthony Appiah draws attention to a striking inconsistency in Sullivan's case for gay marriage. The central distinction Sullivan makes in *Virtually Normal* is between the public realm, where discrimination has no place, and the private realm, where discrimination must be tolerated. But, Appiah asks, is not marriage properly a private relationship? Why should the state have any say in the decision of two people to enter into a permanent sexual, romantic, and domestic arrangement? If Sullivan were fully consistent, in other words, he ought to be arguing not to extend the state's recognition of marriage to gays "but against state recognition of marriage at all."

Like Bruce Bawer, Sullivan insists that gay marriage is a profoundly conservative idea, which by rights ought to appeal to the constituency most worried about how to tame gay behavior. "A law institutionalizing gay marriage," he writes, "would merely reinforce a healthy trend. Burkean conservatives should warm to the idea." Some of his radical critics agree, and for that very reason they take a dim view of the idea. Yet the curious fact remains that gay marriage doesn't *feel* conservative. On the contrary, the thought of it makes conservatives' skin crawl, and they have launched a national campaign to outlaw even the prospect that gays and lesbians might be allowed to wed. Gay marriage is such a fascinating and contentious topic precisely because it can be construed as either deeply reactionary or deeply subversive. Its opponents occupy both ends of the political spectrum.

IV

Sullivan's view of gay sexuality is complicated, even to the point of incoherence. As we have just seen, one of his arguments for gay marriage is that it will reduce promiscuity. In advancing this case, he seems to accept the conservative charge that homosexuals lead depraved lives, "in which emotional commitments are fleeting, promiscuous sex is common, disease is rampant, social ostracism is common, and standards of public decency, propriety and self-restraint are flaunted [he means flouted]." Indeed, he believes that most gay men suffer from a "libidinal pathology" that makes them incapable of sustaining relationships of genuine intimacy. But he refuses to follow Bruce Bawer in denouncing promiscuity as an absolute evil whose reckless pursuit has been the downfall of modern gay culture. On the contrary, he has a healthy respect for the attractions of sexual adventuring as well as an understanding of the historical and psychological factors that have led so many gay men to make this choice. Thus, while he stands to the right of his fellow gay conservatives on most political questions, his sexual opinions are decidedly to the left of the conservative mainstream. The tension between his political and sexual views makes him a more complex (and, frankly, more interesting) figure than Bawer, whose conservatism, by contrast, is both more consistent and less anguished.

Several circumstances have conspired, Sullivan argues, to incline gay men to promiscuity. First and perhaps most fundamental is the brute matter of numbers: because homosexuals constitute only between 2 and 5 percent of the population, pursuing anonymous or promiscuous sex has a kind of statistical logic. "It's as if the hard lessons of adolescence lower permanently—by the sheer dint of the odds—the aspiration for anything more." Another powerful inducement to promiscuity is repression. Because gays grow up being told that their deepest desires can't be realized, they feel a more pressing need for sexual intimacy and relief than do straights, "which is why many gay men approach sex with a reverence and a passion their heterosexual counterparts often misplace somewhere in their adulthood." Furthermore, when society condemns all expressions of homosexuality as equally vile, there is no incentive to choose gay fidelity over gay philandering. Conservatives may be right to consider gay life depraved, but they fail to see how their own categorical condemnations are in some significant degree responsible for the depravity. They have been abetted by gay liberationists who "promoted the tragic lie that no avenue of sexuality was any better or nobler than any other [and] that all demands for responsibility or fidelity or commitment or even healthier psychological integration were mere covers for 'neo-conservatism' or, worse, 'self-hatred.' " Sullivan also suggests that sex holds a greater charm for gays than for straights because their first sexual experience is usually delayed and hence more intoxicating when it finally occurs. Where straights stumble gradually into the pleasures of intimacy, gays often have sex for the first time—and suddenly—as adults, and the experience is so ecstatic that it destroys their psychological equilibrium. "Sometimes I wonder," Sullivan speculates, "whether some homosexuals' addiction to constant romance, to the thrill of the new lover, to the revelation of a new and obliviating desire, is in fact an attempt to relive this experience, again and again."

Temperamentally Sullivan is much closer to the sexual radicals (who are his fiercest critics) than he is to a fellow conservative like Bawer. He is a man who has felt the power of sex and who recognizes that there is nothing else like it. In the midst of his political tract, he frequently risks bathos in an effort to capture the ecstasy of erotic fulfillment. "To physically invade another person, and to be invaded, to merge with another body, to abandon the distance that makes our everyday lives a constant approximation to loneliness, these experiences have never ceased to awe me." Nor does he pretend that desire can be readily confined to a single object. On the contrary, even as he champions marital monogamy as a worthy goal for gay men, he acknowledges his powerful attraction to male bodies. "I still find myself marveling at the exotic beauty of other men," he writes, "at the literally unbelievable sense of having them, finding myself liberated once again by the memory of this puerile joy." No one would ever suspect Andrew Sullivan of having an anemic libido, as one sometimes does with Bruce Bawer. His commitment to gay marriage represents a dramatic sacrifice of his inclinations. Indeed, that commitment is more theoretical than practical, as he has found it virtually impossible to bring his own sexual behavior into line with the goal of monogamy.

Sullivan's sexual ambivalence is evident in his reaction to the cultural phenomenon known as the "circuit," a series of weekend parties held in cities across the country and attended by thousands of gay men, most of them young and buff. The parties are devoted to dancing, drugs, and sex, not all of it protected. They emerged in the 1990s as a reaction (most analysts say) against the sexual shutdown brought on by AIDS, and they have been denounced, by Michelangelo Signorile among others, for promoting behavior that could well reinvigorate the epidemic. In his essay "When Plagues End" (revised and expanded in *Love Undetectable*), Sullivan recounts attending one of these events, the Black Party in Manhattan, along with, he estimates, some six thousand other gay men. He gives a surprisingly even-handed, even sympathetic, account of the experience. To be sure, he fears the circuit represents "another spasm of libidinal pathology" and he complains (as might Bruce Bawer) about "the physical shallowness and emotional cowardice" of the partiers. But he is nonetheless mesmerized by their beauty and clearly sympathizes with their effort to achieve a sense of solidarity in the face of loss through the "crazed physicality" of drugs and sex. So while he can't entirely approve of what he sees, neither will he indulge in the moralistic denunciations of his conservative colleagues. Despite his intellectual commitment to monogamy, he doesn't hold that nonmarital sex is necessarily meaningless and animalistic. "Just because I believe that sex is at its most humane and meaningful and real when it is expressed in love and fidelity," he argues, "it does not follow that I believe that all sex outside such a context is inherently wrong or pernicious." The circuit partiers may be regrettable backsliders, but their behavior, in his view, is comprehensible and more than a little beguiling.

The experience of becoming HIV-positive has only heightened Sullivan's sexual conflictedness. Although he claims to have practiced safe sex and isn't sure how he became infected, he seems to view his disease is a punishment for sexual profligacy. When an old high school friend asked who had infected him, he answered that, because the time between his negative and positive test was more than a year, it could have been anyone. "*Anyone?*" the friend asked incredulously. "How many people did you sleep with, for God's sake?'" To which Sullivan now responds, guiltily, "Too many, God knows. Too many for meaning and dignity to be given to every one; too many for love to be present at each; too many for sex to be very often more than a temporary but powerful release from debilitating fear and loneliness." In *Melancholia and Moralism: Essays on* AIDS *and Queer Politics* (2002) the sex radical and AIDS activist Douglas Crimp cites this "deeply repulsive" remark as a particularly egregious example of Sullivan's moral turpitude, not because he confesses to violating his own monogamous convictions but because he so blithely demeans the worth of sexual experiences of this sort. "How many sex partners are too many?" asks Crimp. "How do you quantify meaning? dignity? love? One can only assume from what Sullivan writes that these qualities *redeem* sex, but do so only in inverse proportion to the number of sex partners. *This* is ethics?"

But while Sullivan clearly regards his philandering as a kind of failure (and a medically consequential one), he does not entirely repudiate it, as Crimp's analysis implies. On the contrary, Sullivan is inclined to excuse his behavior even as he regrets it. He notes that he has never publicly condemned promiscuity, for the very good reason that he feels unable to live up to his own monogamous ideal. "I argued instead," he writes, "for the ennobling and critical institution of marriage," which, over time, would make fidelity no more illusory for gays than it is for straights. But the current generation, he implies, is doomed. He views himself as entirely representative of that generation. He desperately hoped to find someone with whom to form a permanent alliance, but he was unable to do so: "I longed for a relationship that could . . . channel sex into love and commitment and responsibility, but, for whatever reasons, I didn't find it. Instead, I celebrated and articulated its possibility, and did everything I could to advance the day when such relationships could become the norm. But in the meantime, I struggled, and failed, and struggled again." The excuse—that he really wanted to get married but the right guy didn't materialize so he continued to sleep around—sounds vaguely self-deceiving. One sometimes gets the impression that Sullivan's moralizing intelligence tells him one thing while his body tells him another.

His apology for promiscuity is at once melancholy and minimalist. It admits that philandering is reprehensible but implies that so long as gays are damaged goods their sexual misbehavior is to be excused.

Once gay marriage is accepted, we can anticipate that homosexuals will recover from their "libidinal pathology." Their ability to sustain faithful relationships will then be equal to straights' (which of course is far from perfect), and they will achieve a comparable degree of psychological equipoise. Elsewhere, however, Sullivan takes a less "optimistic" view of the homosexual predicament and suggests that gays will always be different. Even under the most tolerant of conditions, they are likely to be less monogamous than straights. Accordingly, he criticizes his fellow conservatives for trying to transform gays into sexual paragons. "There is something baleful," he writes, "about the attempt of some gay conservatives to educate homosexuals and lesbians into an uncritical acceptance of a stifling model of heterosexual normality. The truth is, homosexuals are not entirely normal, and to flatten their varied and complicated lives into a single, moralistic model is to miss what is essential and exhilarating about their otherness." Gays are virtually normal, except when they're not.

Sullivan's apology for gay promiscuity, however tepid, has not escaped the critical eye of straight conservatives. William Bennett in particular has charged him with advocating gay "adultery." Bennett's case rests on a line in the epilogue to *Virtually Normal* where Sullivan suggests that gay marriages might prove more supple than straight marriages in addressing the desire for sexual variety: "There is more likely to be greater understanding of the need for extramarital outlets between two men than between a man and a woman." Sullivan has tried to deflect the criticism by charging that the line was taken out of context and that Bennett "ignores the two central chapters of my book—and several articles—in which I unequivocally argue for monogamy as central to all marriage, same-sex or opposite sex." In a more recent essay, "We Are All Sodomites Now," Sullivan offers a more full-voiced defense of sexual expression beyond the bounds of marital monogamy: "It is hard to see why . . . sexual fantasy, escape, pleasure are somehow inimical to human flourishing—and plenty of evidence that their permanent or too-rigid suppression does actual psychological and spiritual harm. Relationships which include sexual adventure and passion and experiment are not relationships of 'disintegrated' people, but relationships in which trust is the prerequisite for relief, release and renewal." It is difficult to escape the conclusion that Sullivan remains deeply divided about gay sexuality. The fact that he has come under attack from both the sexual right and the sexual left—from William Bennett on the one hand, and Douglas Crimp on the other—testifies to the instability of his views. He's a theoretical puritan but a temperamental libertine.

v

Sullivan has turned to friendship as an alternative to love. Gay friendship is the subject of a long essay, "If Love Were All," in his second book, *Love Undetectable*. The essay is a meditation on the place of friendship in gay life (and its articulation in Western thought) as well as an account of his own friendship with a young man named Patrick, who died of AIDS. Sullivan presents his thinking about friendship as profoundly shaped by the experience of the epidemic, which is the subject of another essay in *Love Undetectable*, "When Plagues End." But I would suggest that his enthusiasm for friendship is also a product of the difficulties he has encountered in the sexual realm. Because he has been unable to reconcile his romantic ideals with the rude reality of his desires, he has turned to friendship as a kind of unproblematic alternative. It engages the heart, as does love, but for the most part leaves the body unaffected. In friendship he has found the harmonious and untroubled bond to another human being that has eluded him in the world of romance. Friendship, one might say, is a safe harbor for the gay man whose anarchic sexual impulses are at odds with his monogamous aspirations.

That friendship has become a substitute for love is suggested by the history of Sullivan's relationship with Patrick. It began, Sullivan confesses, with his falling in love with the young man, who recommended himself not just for the usual erotic reasons but because he shared Sullivan's political views: "Both of us were dogged traditionalists, revering ancient writers and classical composers, bored if not amused by academic fashion, skeptical of politics, enraged by the idiocy of much of what passed for gay activism." They were also both Roman Catholics who refused to leave the Church despite its official homophobia. On their first date they got drunk and stuffed themselves—which seemed a promising overture to romance—but in the event the "courtship" quickly collapsed. Significantly, we learn that Patrick, for all his ideological conservatism, was a sexual adventurer: he saw no necessary incompatibility between romance and sexual experimenting, and at the time of their meeting he was involved with more than one other man. Sullivan reports the fact without so much as a hint of rebuke. His unabashed admiration for this Lothario is further evidence of his own less than perfect commitment to monogamy.

Where love failed, friendship flourished, and Sullivan is eager to argue that, far from being second best or faute de mieux, friendship is better than love. Indeed, he argues that friendship is the great gay achievement. Sexually and romantically, gays and straights are more alike than different. But in their capacity for friendship gays have proved themselves to be "unequaled," manifestly so in the wake of the AIDS epidemic. Sullivan thus takes issue with Frank Browning's characterization of gay culture as a "culture of desire": "What gay culture really is before it is anything else, before it is a culture of desire or a culture of subversion or a culture of pain, is a culture of friendship." He argues the case for friendship's superiority with Proustian rigor. Romantic love may be overwhelming, but it doesn't last. Like Swann, he observes that while love "can eclipse every other emotion and transport us to levels of bliss and communion we have never felt before," its dissolution is inexorable. Friendship, though less intense, is vastly more reliable. Even Sullivan's most hostile critics claim to be moved by his account of the friendship with Patrick, which they apparently can't reconcile with their general picture of him as, in Michelangelo Signorile's words, a "nasty, dishonest pundit." But I sense more than a whiff of sour grapes in his encomium: love hasn't worked out, so he has settled for friendship. His entire effort to set love at odds with friendship—to contend that "the great modern enemy of friendship has turned out to be love"—seems an obvious rationalization for his romantic misadventures.

Sullivan's discussion of his friendship with Patrick raises the more general issue of the place of self-revelation in his writings. As with Bruce Bawer, autobiography figures prominently in his case for gay conservatism, both in the expressly personal essays gathered in *Love Undetectable* and in the more cerebral, even academic, argument of *Virtually Normal*. But where Bawer is a naïve autobiographer Sullivan is a sentimental one. I draw on Schiller's famous distinction to suggest that Bawer's self-revelations are generally artless, while Sullivan displays himself in a highly self-conscious fashion. His particular style of autobiography might be described as "manipulative vulnerability": he exposes his weaknesses, then strikes with ferocity. Put another way, he represents a curious combination of the fragile sufferer and the bully. There is a powerful narcissism at work here: he loves to talk about himself, especially in embarrassing ways, which somehow excuses the naked aggression of his assaults on those who disagree with him. Surely, we think, no one who has endured such pain and revealed such failings could be a ruthless hater. But in fact the self-abnegation, however authentic, disguises an even more profound self-assertion.

By recounting the agony of growing up homosexual Sullivan clearly intends to shame his conservative readers into recognizing the inhumanity of their prejudice. Already as a child he anticipated disaster: "My mother remembers an incident I have subsequently forgotten. When I was only eight, I came to her and asked if God really knew everything about you, if He could see into every part of you and know exactly what you were thinking and feeling. Yes, she replied. 'Then there's no hope for me, Mum,' I apparently said, and walked back into my bedroom, despondent." A prepubescent crush on a "handsome and effortlessly athletic" boy provided him with his introduction to "the homosexual hurt that is the accompaniment of homosexual lives." Later his longings became so intense that he found himself compulsively drawing sketches of the men he desired and cutting out pictures of male models from magazines. His reaction to his predicament wasn't entirely negative. Rather he felt a mixture of exhilaration and disgust, though the dominant emotion was despair, particularly at the prospect of being excluded from romance and marriage, the obvious life goals of his peers. He also developed a series of neurotic disorders, "washing my hands and feet compulsively, carefully avoiding cracks in the sidewalk, compulsively vacuuming the house, cleaning the kitchen, tidying my room." Perhaps most tellingly, he compensated for his catastrophic defect by honing his intellectual skills, becoming a star debater, and fantasizing about a grandiose future as "a prime minister or war leader." In other words, he cultivated precisely the talents that were to serve him so well as a polemicist. But at a very high price. He bristled with defense mechanisms, including affected speech and outlandish dress, and suffered a complete emotional shutdown. "For years," he confesses, "I lived sexually and emotionally in a world of fantasy, masturbation, and self-contained shame."

The sense of pain and vulnerability did not end when he had his first homosexual love affair, at twenty-three. To be sure, the experience itself was ecstatic: "It was like being in a black-and-white movie that suddenly converted to color. The richness of experience seemed possible for the first time; the abstractions of dogma, of morality, of society, dissolved into the sheer, mysterious pleasure of being human." (The somewhat hackneyed *Wizard of Oz* metaphor is deployed more systematically by Arnie Kantrowitz in his autobiography, *Under the Rainbow: Growing Up Gay*.) But the self-disgust was not entirely banished and returned with a vengeance when he received his HIV diagnosis seven years later, just before he turned thirty. He was, he discovered, still ashamed: "Even then—even in me, someone who had thought and worked and struggled to banish the stigma and the guilt and the fear of my homosexuality—I instinctively interpreted this illness as something that I deserved. Its arrival obliterated all that carefully constructed confidence in my own self-worth. It showed me in a flash how so much of that achievement had been illusory—how, in a pinch, I still loathed and feared an inextricable part of who I was." He struggled to overcome this initial response and eventually convinced himself that the disease was a godsend, although he expresses his newfound confidence in a curiously reticent and (literally) parenthetical way: "I began to see the condition not as something constricting

ITHACA COLLEGE LIBRARY

but as something liberating—liberating because it forced me to confront more profoundly than ever before whether or not my sexuality
was something shameful (I became convinced that it was not)." Even
when the arrival of protease inhibitors emboldened him to proclaim
his (and his generation's) triumph over the disease, he soon found
himself sinking into "a yawning depression," as a sense of "muffling"
sadness reasserted itself. Clearly the burden of homophobia and the
fear of a shameful and early death continue to haunt him, if only subconsciously. I suspect that the bombastic and loutish manner of his
political writing (especially about Iraq) represents an effort keep his
feelings of self-disgust and anxiety from resurfacing. Abjection is an
ever-present threat, held at bay only by noisy self-assertiveness.

VI

Sullivan's 1996 *New York Times Magazine* article "When Plagues End"
caused a good deal of outrage. Indeed, the piece was regularly denounced as "infamous." Sullivan professes to have been flabbergasted
by the reaction. "When I first wrote that it was possible to conceive
of the end of the plague," he observes, "the response among many
gay men was so publicly hostile it took my breath away." But in private he heard just the opposite: "AIDS activists who, in the press, be-
rated anyone who ventured optimism confidentially asked each other
what they were going to do with the rest of their lives, now that the
emergency had passed." I should confess that I've never understood
the hostility Sullivan's essay provoked. Perhaps his enthusiasm for
protease inhibitors revealed a certain lack of compassion for those
who were too sick to benefit from them, just as it may have under-
estimated the side effects—and in some cases outright failure—of
the new drugs. But his main point seems incontrovertible: for the
majority of sufferers the new combination therapy transformed what
had been a death sentence into a manageable illness. Equally unde-
niable is that an overwhelming sense of relief swept through the gay
community almost overnight. Significantly, Sullivan's analysis is supported by the sex radical Eric Rofes, whose book, *Dry Bones Breathe:*

Gay Men Creating Post-AIDS Identities and Cultures (1998), announces, "AIDS, as we have known it, *is* over." Nor is it plausible to argue that Sullivan's optimism about the disease was somehow inspired by his conservatism. On the contrary, as the mention of Rofes suggests, it actually put him in league with the sexual left in so far as his upbeat assessment opened up the possibility for a reassertion of gay eroticism.

One can't overstate the importance of AIDS and the recovery from AIDS in Sullivan's life. Although it didn't change his politics, it transformed him in human terms. Above all, it gave him a powerful sense of solidarity with other sufferers, producing intense friendships and no less intense feelings of loss. He put himself in the trenches of the epidemic, at one point helping a mortally ill stranger with "constant, uncontrollable diarrhea." His harrowing accounts of friends and lovers sickening and dying before his eyes convey a sense of genuine emotion untainted by the self-consciousness that mars so much of his autobiographical writing. In this respect, he is very much an insider, deeply embedded in the central experience of his generation of gay men. Bruce Bawer, whose greater natural chastity probably saved him from AIDS, by contrast remains something of an outsider. Interestingly, Bawer has abandoned America for Europe, while Sullivan, the born Brit, has cultivated an almost frightening sense of identification with America and all things American.

Like most conservatives, Sullivan argues that the great achievement of the epidemic has been to awaken gays to a sense of responsibility. AIDS forced them to recognize the childishness of the liberationist ideals that had dominated their lives since the 1970s. This new sense of responsibility won gays heretofore unknown respect from the straight community and, he believes, set the table for the military and marriage issues that came to dominate gay politics in the 1990s: "Once gay men had experienced beyond any doubt the fiber of real responsibility—the responsibility for life and death for themselves and others—more and more found it impossible to acquiesce in second-class lives. They demanded full recognition of their service to their country, and equal treatment under the law for the relationships they had cherished and sustained in the teeth of such terror." For all its horrors, in other words, AIDS dramatically improved the moral and political situation in which gays found themselves.

Sullivan's recovery from HIV seems to be complete. He reports taking twenty-seven pills a day, as a result of which his viral load is now "undetectable." But his new-found health has got him into sexual trouble. He has become a kind of apologist for unprotected intercourse between HIV-positives, which, in turn, has made him a target of criticism for those, like Michelangelo Signorile, who are convinced that such behavior risks a renaissance of the epidemic. In *Love Undetectable* Sullivan gives a highly circumstantial account of a sexual encounter with an old friend who had been HIV-positive for nearly a decade: "As night fell, we found ourselves suddenly, unexpectedly in an embrace that lasted longer than it should have. The relief of survival, the knowledge of survival, was suddenly too much. We found ourselves holding each other almost as if we were all each of us had left, and with a need and a relish that took both of us by surprise. . . . There are times when only bodies can express what minds cannot account for. So we kissed and embraced and clung to each other in silence. And as the passion grew, we found ourselves, without a word between us, taking the embrace still further and still further until, for the first time in each of our lives, as our bodies came together, we did not bother to reach for protection, and intimated in a single, mutual, liberating smile that not even the caution of so many years would bring anything any longer between us. 'Are you sure?' he asked me. 'Yes, I'm sure,' I replied. No other words were necessary. And the barrier broke at last. And the fear was rebuked at last." The passage is perhaps not strictly speaking an "apology" for bareback sex insofar as Sullivan's focus is less on the sheer physical pleasure of unprotected intercourse than on the psychological need for connection after so many years of fear and denial. But it nonetheless justifies, even glamorizes, a raw sexual encounter without any concern for its possible consequences. The passage also occupies a kind of intellectual limbo when considered from the perspective of Sullivan's views about monogamy and promiscuity. While the sex is neither anonymous nor impersonal (and hence, one could argue, not truly promiscuous), there is no suggestion that the two men are at the beginning of a serious romance. On the contrary, we get the firm impression that this is a singular event, a unique celebration of their shared physical and emotional regeneration. Sullivan says nothing about its morality, though the rather ripe language of the final lines invites us to approve of the men's behavior.

A more spectacular example of getting into sexual trouble is the catfight that erupted between Sullivan and Michelangelo Signorile in 2001 when Signorile published an article, "The Contradictory Faces of Andrew Sullivan," accusing Sullivan of advertising for bareback sex on the Web. Under the screen name of "RawMuscleGlutes," Signorile reported, Sullivan had posted headless nude photos of himself and listed his sexual tastes: "He checked off the various boxes: 'I take loads in my ass. I take loads in my mouth. I give loads in asses. I give loads in mouths. My HIV status: Poz. I prefer you to be: Poz. I'm interested in bi scenes. One-on-ones. 3-ways. Groups/Parties/Orgies. Gang Bangs.'" Signorile could barely contain his glee as he drove home the contradiction between Sullivan's official moralistic convictions and his stunningly lax (and, in Signorile's view, dangerous) behavior: "What was jarring . . . was the sheer incongruity between the public persona that many rightly or wrongly perceive as Sullivan's— conservative, moral, devoutly Catholic, marriage-minded, . . . arrogant toward the ghettoized gay scene—and the person depicted on the sites, . . . someone very much in the gay sexual fast lane, all pumped up and describing his 'power glutes,' ravenously eager to hook up but letting prospective partners know that 'no fats, no fems' need apply."

Sullivan defended himself in an essay, "Sexual McCarthyism," which, perhaps significantly, he published as an attachment to his Web site but nowhere in hard print. As a defense it is rather lame, because he is unable to deny the basic truth of the facts. Essentially he accuses Signorile of an unconscionable invasion of privacy motivated by ideological disagreement. In other words, he presents the episode as another example of the gay left out to get him. "This 'story,'" he writes, "was fomented clearly by malice. . . . It was propagated by someone who made no pretense about his political loathing of me, and who has devoted a large part of his career to attacking me." Almost pathetically, he justifies the posting on the grounds that he can't get a date: "It's hard for me to meet men easily. My mini-celebrity often gets in the way of getting to know someone naturally, and personal ads avoid the whole problem of preconceived notions of who I am and what I'm like." He rejects Signorile's accusation that bareback sex is dangerous because it risks reinfection with a new (and potentially deadly) strain of the virus. Because the theory of reinfection is based on a "slim reed of research," Sullivan concludes, "The question of whether to abandon condoms in sex between two self-disclosed HIV positive people is a decision for those two people alone in private."

Several months after "outing" Sullivan as a barebacker, Signorile published a follow-up piece in which he claimed to have received threats from "several gay conservative individuals." "One individual who threatened me with physical violence," he continued, "is in fact a close friend and associate of Sullivan's." Sullivan, so far as I can ascertain, never responded to the charge. Perhaps he didn't consider it his responsibility. More likely, I suspect, he decided that the entire issue was a loser for him. He concluded "Sexual McCarthyism" with the announcement, "This is the last I will say or write on this subject, so save your media calls and e-mails."

The dustup is fascinating, not just because it reveals the extreme nature of Sullivan's sexual predicament but also because it documents the remarkable level of personal antagonism that now characterizes disagreements between gay intellectuals. From the perspective of the Stonewall era, when we were so conscious of our shared history and oppression and our newly discovered ethos of gay brotherhood, the sheer viciousness of the exchange is stunning. Moreover, the contempt with which Sullivan and Signorile address one another has become the norm since the emergence of the new conservatism, as we'll see when we come to consider Sullivan's other gay critics, Richard Goldstein and Michael Warner. Nothing, I think, gives more dramatic evidence of a new era in the history of homosexuality than the personal animosity that gay writers and activists now regularly display toward one another. Of course, from the perspective of the conservatives themselves, the new incivility is not necessarily a bad thing. Rather, it shows that gays have come of age. They no longer feel compelled to maintain a united ideological front. Like any mature and respected constituency within the polity, they can indulge an unfettered airing of their disagreements.

VII

I have suggested that the new gay conservatism has had three main areas of concern: politics, sex, and gender. Andrew Sullivan is the most political of the new conservatives in the sense that his analysis of the homosexual predicament identifies it above all as a political problem and one allowing of political solution. Moreover, the brand of politics he advocates is more conservative than that proposed by any of his colleagues on the gay right. Like all the new conservatives, he is a critic of the alliance politics that have dominated official gay thinking in the past quarter century. Recently, for example, he denounced the National Gay and Lesbian Task Force for taking an official position against the war in Iraq, arguing, as might Bruce Bawer, that "War isn't a gay issue." But no other gay conservative has advanced so extreme a political vision as Sullivan's austere combination of public equality (the right to marry and serve in the military) and private prejudice (no antidiscrimination or hate crime legislation). Politically, he is on the right end of the gay right spectrum.

In his opinions on sex, on the other hand, Sullivan stands to the left of his conservative colleagues, indeed to the left of some thinkers, like Michelangelo Signorile and Gabriel Rotello, who hold much more progressive political views. His theoretical devotion to marriage and monogamy, as we have seen, exists side by side with a track record of sexual indulgence and even a certain conceptual tolerance for erotic adventuring. One cannot imagine him settling down to Bruce Bawer's gay domestic bliss any more than one can imagine Bawer advertising for bareback sex on the Web. To be sure, over the past year or so Sullivan's blog has contained regular allusions to "the boyfriend" (as well as "the dog"), but the irony and impersonality of these allusions imply

Andrew Sullivan and His Enemies   79

something less than the wholehearted romantic devotion that Bawer exemplifies.

What about gender? For the most part, gay conservatives advocate an unalloyed masculinism that rejects all public displays of effeminacy (such as one sees in Gay Pride parades) or any show of political solidarity with gender deviants and transsexuals. Gay men, conservatives argue, are naturally as masculine as straight men, just as lesbians are naturally as feminine as straight women. More precisely, to the extent that effeminacy and mannishness exist, they are viewed as the pathological byproducts of the repression under which homosexuals have lived, and they will wither away when that oppression is ended. In effect, gay conservatives envision a world in which gender will no longer be a gay issue.

Sullivan's ideas about gender are more complex. If he stands to the political right but the sexual left of his fellow gay conservatives, he is somewhere in the gender middle. Admittedly, he has a high tolerance for butchness and presents himself very much as a man's man, without so much as a trace of girlishness or camp. He has written—infamously, some would say—celebrating the virtues of testosterone. He is also a fan of the new evolutionary psychology, with its "findings" about the biologically rooted differences between the sexes, in particular, the greater natural promiscuousness of men. Indeed, he is inclined to see a good deal of gay male behavior as the inevitable result of male biological urges untrammeled by the company of women: "The most likely explanation for certain kinds of sexual pathologies—particularly those related to promiscuity, sexual objectification, and persistent sexual dissatisfaction—is that male homosexual society is, well, male."

Sullivan's masculinism expresses itself in a number of particular opinions. For example, he is fond of arguing that gay men have much less in common with lesbians than they do with straight men. "My own view," he writes, "is that . . . gender differences, if anything, are deeper than the differences between heterosexuals and homosexuals. Which is to say that lesbian culture is always likely to be far more estranged from gay male culture than heterosexual culture, and vice versa." Sometimes he suggests that lesbians offer an example of couplehood and fidelity that gay men ought to emulate. But he more consistently argues that lesbians and gays—because they are women and men, respectively—are differently coded and given to different styles of relationship: "If anything, lesbian relationships sometimes suffer from a surfeit of intimacy and commitment, occasionally breaking down because the women involved overwhelm each other with mutual concern and enmeshment. If homosexual pathology is defined as an inability to bond in a stable relation, then lesbianism, and not psychoanalysis, might seem to be the 'cure.'" I should note that many lesbians—or at least lesbian intellectuals—resent this condescending effort to place them on a sexual pedestal.

Sullivan's masculinism also helps explain his passion for gays in the military. The truth is he thinks gays are natural soldiers, whose inherent manliness and aggression will find ideal expression in the military. "Of all institutions in our society," he writes, "the military is perhaps the most naturally homosexual, which is part of the reason, of course, why it is so hostile to their visible presence." The Greek legend of the Sacred Band of Thebes, who fought so bravely because they were homosexual lovers, lies behind this conception, though it also draws on images of other putatively gay soldiers like Achilles and Patroclus or Alexander the Great. It expects that the heroic performance of out gays in the military will retire forever the image of the effeminate homosexual, too frivolous and self-absorbed for the manly responsibilities of combat. Clearly, Sullivan relishes the day when gays can reclaim their birthright as society's natural warriors, just as they banish the memory of their depraved history as drag queens and draft dodgers. The exact opposite values and concerns explain why many gay radicals have mixed feelings about the military issue: they agree that the ban is unjust, but they hate the idea of gays being corrupted by the military's ugly male chauvinism and its fondness for foreign adventure. Born in the era of the Vietnam War protests, the gay movement originally stood against everything the military represented. That the right to serve (alongside the right to marry) should have become the centerpiece of gay politics is deeply dispiriting for the aging adepts of Gay Liberation. Sullivan, by contrast, is as devoted to military glory as any red-blooded American boy raised on computer games and sports. His delight in the American military performance in Iraq was unqualified.

Sullivan is not above indulging in the cheap misogyny of other gay conservatives, as when he charges that the National Gay and Lesbian Task Force is a hotbed of political correctness because it has had a series of female heads (among them, his critic Urvashi Vaid). But he is equally capable of expressing sympathy for certain feminist issues, for example, in his harsh criticism of the Roman Catholic Church for excluding women from the priesthood. Moreover, despite his general hostility to alliance politics, he, in contrast to most gay conservatives, is able to recognize a structural link between misogyny and homophobia and hence he can acknowledge that gays have an interest in the equality of women. "Toleration for gay bashers or of hostility to effeminate homosexuals," he writes, "implies toleration of wife beating and contempt for women." Elsewhere he gives the structural connection between gay and women's issues a distinctly conservative inflection: "If young men and women were taught in childhood to respect the few among their midst who were homosexual, . . . it might also be beneficial for inculcating in young men a respect for women that is conducive to responsible courtship and successful marriage." Although hardly remarkable, such sentiments are seldom heard on the gay right.

Similarly, Sullivan is not obsessed with effeminate homosexuals to anything like the same degree as Bruce Bawer. Sometimes he mouths the conservative wisdom that gender deviance is a pathological product of repression, as when he laments the "excessive masculinity or caricatured femininity" to which gay men are sometimes driven by their "early wounds." But, unlike other conservatives, he is capable of admiring the political efficacy of a certain kind of camp, as in his salute to "a gaggle of homosexuals in large-brimmed hats" at the 1993 march on Washington carrying a sign, " 'Gays in the Millinery.' " In general he likes to present himself as comfortable in the presence of gender-benders, even appreciative of their historical achievement, though he finally patronizes them as having sacrificed their dignity to the cause. "These extraordinary products of a long history of isolation and marginalization," he writes, "are marvels of revolt, of invention, and, often, of beauty. Insofar as they are inventive products of a culture of energetic difference, symbols of a determination to survive against considerable odds, they merit an intense admiration and defense. But insofar as these cultural expressions are also products of a deep and searing anxiety, of the inability to be publicly a gay man or woman except as a caricature of one gender or another, then they are no more to be clung to than excruciating racial stereotypes." The implication, at the end, that drag queens and diesel dykes are the gay equivalent of Sambo can hardly be considered an endorsement, but, however ambivalent and condescending, his acknowledgment of the heroism of gender nonconformists puts him at odds with his fellow gay conservatives. Richard Goldstein is convinced that Sullivan harbors a deep contempt for queens. "He's appalled by camping, prancing, or any expression of effeminacy," writes Goldstein. But that characterization suits Bruce Bawer far better than Sullivan, who, I'm inclined to think, is a more supple masculinist than Goldstein gives him credit for. His thinking about gender may not be so tortured and contradictory as his thinking about sex, but it is less consistently reactionary than his thinking about politics.

VIII

Andrew Sullivan's emergence in the 1990s as the most visible advocate of gay conservatism has prompted three book-length responses from the gay left: Urvashi Vaid's *Virtual Equality: The Mainstreaming of Gay and Lesbian Liberation* (1995), Michael Warner's *The Trouble with Normal: Sex, Politics, and the Ethics of Queer Life* (1999), and Richard Goldstein's *The Attack Queers: Liberal Media and the Gay Right* (2002). Uvashi Vaid's book is perhaps not technically a response to Sullivan since it appeared the same year as *Virtually Normal*. But, as its title implies, it is at least in part an answer to the view to homosexual politics advanced by Sullivan, notably in the 1993 *New Republic* article that adumbrated the argument of his book. Vaid's *Virtual Equality* might be described as a response from the institutional gay left and its organizations, like the National Gay and Lesbian Task Force, of which she was public information director and executive director from 1986 to 1992. Michael Warner's critique, by contrast, comes from the camp of sex radicals, who are as hostile to the national institutions as they are to self-confessed conservatives like Sullivan. Finally, Richard Goldstein, who is a generation older than Vaid or Warner, assaults Sullivan from the historical perspective of the Gay Liberation movement.

The "virtual" that seems to link Andrew Sullivan's *Virtually Normal* and Urvashi Vaid's *Virtual Equality* turns out to have quite different connotations. For Sullivan "virtual" means something like "for all practical purposes": he presents himself—and other homosexuals like him—as sharing the same values and aspirations as the American mainstream, and he argues that his sexual orientation, while it is obviously important and separates him from the vast majority of the population, is ultimately an inconsequential anomaly. The thrust of *Virtually Normal* is that an ever increasing number of gays are—for all practical purposes—indistinguishable from their fellow citizens. The "virtual" in Vaid's *Virtual Equality*, by contrast, means something like "apparent" or "inauthentic." Vaid's intention is just the opposite of Sullivan's. She argues that the progress of gays toward equality has been more apparent than real. "We are freer than we were in the 1940s and 1960s" she concedes, "but we have failed to realize true equality or win full acceptance as moral human beings." Moreover, the emergence of gay intellectuals like Sullivan and Bawer, who argue that assimilation has succeeded, creates the danger that gays will accept their subordinate situation as the equivalent of full and equal citizenship. The purpose of *Virtual Equality* is to call attention to that continuing subordination and offer remedies for it.

Quite unfairly, the *New York Times Book Review* invited Bruce Bawer to review *Virtual Equality* when it appeared in 1995. He gave it a predictable thumbs down. He dismisses Vaid as a relic of the gay movement's ideological past, out of touch with the ever more moderate and assimilated gay mainstream that wants no part of her proposed "social, economic and political revolution." The judgment is both unjust and unobservant. There is no talk of "revolution" in *Virtual Equality*. Its program is the mildest sort of progressive gradualism. Indeed, what is striking about the book is precisely the degree to which it retreats from confrontation and advocates a kind of coalition politics in which the voices of gay conservatives will be heard right alongside those of gay radicals. In other words, *Virtual Equality* offers eloquent, if unintended, evidence of the deradicalization of the gay movement. Even as it urges gays to resist a premature embrace of their second-class citizenship, it betrays, especially in its cautious and accommodating language, an intense awareness of the changed political landscape of the 1990s. Urvashi Vaid is very much a chastened revolutionary.

At its heart *Virtual Equality* is a defense of alliance politics. It argues that gays will never achieve full equality in a society that remains racist and sexist. In her more radical moments Vaid extends her indictment to include economic injustice as well. "Gay civil rights," she argues, "must be seen as part of a broader focus on human rights, sexual and gender equality, social and economic justice, and faith in a multiracial society." She is never very specific about what she means by "social and economic justice." Bawer accuses her of advocating revolutionary socialism. But nothing in her text supports that charge. Rather, like nearly everyone else on the left since the fall of Communism, she seems to accept the inevitability of capitalism. She simply urges the gay movement to side with progressives on the various issues before the nation: "The deficit, crime, public schools, housing, the role of government, national defense, welfare reform, and the shrinkage of the workforce—are all national issues that the gay movement has failed to address. We must end this silence and develop a movement courageous enough to articulate gay liberation's approaches to these broad social crises."

Over and over in *Virtual Equality* Vaid advances a rhetorical case for alliance politics. "We argue," she writes in a characteristic passage, "that our movement must deal with race, gender, and class, along with sexual orientation." But nowhere in her overlong book does she mount anything resembling an argument for the alliance ideal. She complains that gay intellectuals have failed to "articulate clearly how sexual identity, race, gender, and economic realities [are] interconnected." But she herself offers not even a gesture toward such an "articulation." There is no analysis of the structural links between the oppression of gays and the oppression of women, minorities, and the poor. Similarly, there is no effort to show the intellectual or discursive affiliation of homophobia with racism and sexism. Instead of mounting an argument she falls back on subjective autobiographical evidence, as when she asserts, "I will never be convinced that racial and gender issues belong in some 'other' movement; they are fused in my body with my lesbianism, and I reject single identity-based politics." In effect, she fails to give us any reason to choose her ideal of a coalition of the oppressed over Bawer's insistence on single-issue purity. Her striking inability to argue her case—as opposed simply to asserting it—drastically undermines the effectiveness of her polemic and suggests a failure of nerve

Vaid of course knows that the ideal of coalition politics has been challenged by the new gay right. Faced with this internal opposition, her inclination is not to denounce the renegades but rather to acknowledge their existence and report their views in innocuously neutral language. Her evenhanded manner in effect concedes that alliance politics has lost the authority it once enjoyed. She seems fully resigned to the more contested political universe in which gay progressives now find themselves. The mood of *Virtual Equality* is decidedly Thermadorian.

A striking illustration of Vaid's deradicalization is provided by her account of a conversation with Andrew Sullivan on the subject of racism and homophobia: "At a gay and lesbian retreat we both attended, Andrew Sullivan and I discussed the involvement of the gay movement in racial justice. I argued that tackling racism was inherently important for the gay movement for two reasons: because it was the right thing to do, and because a large number of gay and lesbian people are people of color. I maintained that antiracist work was integral to our work against homophobia because the same forces in society justified both forms of prejudice, and because gay people as a minority need allies in order to win politically. Andrew disagreed. He said that what I described made the gay and lesbian movement sound like a subset of a broader racial justice movement. While he had no quarrel with such an antiracist movement, he thought our gay movement needed to stay focused on gay and lesbian issues alone. He was uncomfortable with broadening the movement on pragmatic grounds, because not everyone in the gay community was committed to racial justice." And the argument stops right there. The two adversarial positions are simply juxtaposed, with no effort to show that one is superior to the other. Such a muted and unresolved confrontation leaves the impression that Vaid has lost the courage of her convictions. Likewise, the familiar and decorous manner of her encounter with "Andrew" implies that his views deserve as much respect as her own. (Elsewhere she praises the "great eloquence and urgency" of Sullivan's journalistic pieces on the gays-in-the-military issue.) The posture she adopts here utterly belies Bawer's portrait of her as a diehard revolutionary. Rather, she comes across as a cautious pluralist who accepts the reality of the gay world's politically divided allegiances.

The same deradicalized perspective informs Vaid's account of the history of the gay movement in this country. Like most students of the topic, she sees the movement divided between "legitimationists" who pursue a limited civil rights agenda and "liberationists" who view the achievement of gay freedom and equality as part of a much broader social transformation. Vaid's heart is with the liberationists. "A liberation movement seeks fundamental social change," she writes; "we are for a just world in which racism, homophobia, sexism, economic injustice, and other systems of domination are frankly addressed and replaced with new models." But she makes no effort to argue for the liberationist position. Rather, as in her discussion of alliance politics and its critics, she gives a tediously evenhanded account of the struggle between the two principles. Once again we get the clear impression that the ascendancy of gay conservatives in the 1990s has forced her to move to the political center. She ends her analysis with a typically cautious, indeed banal, judgment that the two traditions are actually "compatible" and that whether one works for gay civil rights or for a systematic transformation of society is ultimately a matter of individual taste: "A more productive way for us to move beyond the dialectic of liberation and legitimation is to acknowledge that neither 'side' is wrong, and support each other where we can." As this innocuous bromide attests, Vaid's radicalism has been thoroughly eviscerated.

A similar caution is evident in her relatively limited comments on the two issues, besides politics, that have figured prominently in the gay-right critique of gay culture, gender nonconformity and sexual expressiveness. Against the conservatives—Bruce Bawer in particular—she puts in a good word for drag queens. Her defense, however, is not on the principled ground that they pose a radical challenge to the established gender order and its inequities, as Judith Butler has argued, but rather that they are reliable financial contributors to gay causes. "It bears repeating," she writes, "that drag performers have played an enormous role in grassroots fundraising for gay and lesbian projects. The Imperial Court of America, a nationwide network of drag activists, raises tens of thousands of dollars for AIDS and gay and lesbian charities each year." Admirable, to be sure, but of no conceptual consequence. Similarly, Vaid wants to side with the prosex contingent in the gay sex wars, noting that as a writer at *Gay Community News* in the 1980s (alongside Michael Bronski) she argued against closing the bathhouses. But her natural proclivity is, again, to adopt an implicitly centrist position, reporting on the views advanced by each side but taking no position of her own. Thus she observes, without comment, "Progressive gay men feel so committed to the ideal of post-Stonewall, pre-AIDS, libertine sexuality that they rarely listen to criticism offered by other gay men that baths and commercial sex clubs feel degrading to them. Such talk is dismissed as antisexual or is treated as a challenge to their idealized notions of unfettered gay male sexuality." Though not a prude, she shows no great enthusiasm for sex. On the contrary, the subject makes her squeamish. She complains, for example, that homophobes like to harp on the sexual aspect of homosexual lives: "In every public utterance, they attempt to reinforce the association of homosexuality with sexuality, by talking graphically about anal sex, sexually transmitted diseases, and particular practices like oral sex, rimming, and water sports." Michael Warner would recognize this discomfort with gay sexual practices as characteristically reactionary. Vaid prefers to defend "pleasure, joy, and desire" rather than anything so vivid and specific as "rimming and water sports."

In sum, *Virtual Equality* offers only the most tepid criticism of the new gay right. Rather than a vigorous defense of the traditional progressive ideals of the gay movement, it preaches a mushy accommodation of conservative and moderate views. Like the "big tent" Republican centrists, Vaid invites gays of all political stripes to participate in the movement without concern for ideological consistency or even coherence. The only group she would exclude is the pedophiles, whom she doesn't consider "part of homosexual identity" and casts aside as brutally as Bruce Bawer himself. However unintentionally, her book is as much a tribute to the newly acquired clout of gay conservatives as it is a defense of the familiar agenda of the gay left.

IX

The most forcible and incisive critic of Andrew Sullivan's views, especially about gay marriage, is the scholar Michael Warner. Warner is a professor of English at Rutgers and the author of the admired study, *The Letters of the Republic: Publication and the Public Sphere in Eighteenth-century America*. In 1999 he took time from his usual academic duties to publish *The Trouble with Normal*, which, as the title implies, is an attack on Sullivan's ideas and arguments in *Virtually Normal*. Warner calls the book "a non-academic work of political polemic." In contrast to Urvashi Vaid's half-hearted and deeply compromised defense of the progressive gay agenda, *The Trouble with Normal* is an unembarrassed apology for the most radical and disruptive vision of queer life.

Warner disputes Sullivan's contention that homosexuals are or want to be "normal." The idea of normality, in the sense of conforming to the statistical average, has, he insists, "no moral value."

Furthermore, embracing normality is always an invidious gesture: one proclaims oneself normal in order to "throw shame on those who stand farther down the ladder of respectability." Thus the real purpose of Sullivan's celebration of gay normality, in Warner's view, is to cast into outer darkness anyone who fails to measure up in terms of gender presentation and, especially, sexual behavior: "the queers who have sex in public toilets, who don't 'come out' as happily gay, the sex workers, the lesbians who are too vocal about their taste for dildos or S/M, the boys who flaunt it as pansies or as leathermen, the androgynes, the trannies or transgendered whose gender deviance makes them unassimilable to the menu of sexual orientations, the clones in the so-called gay ghetto, the fist-fuckers and popper-snorters, the ones who actually like pornography." In effect, Warner accuses Sullivan of betraying all those who don't conform to his bourgeois standards of manliness and sexual propriety. Sullivan celebrates "good gays" and denigrates "bad queers." Warner is proud to count himself one of the "bad queers" whose behavior is under attack by the new gay right. His book is a defense of the sexual lumpenproletariat.

Warner is convinced that Sullivan's deepest impulse is the desire to desexualize homosexuals. He ignores the evidence that Sullivan's actual feelings about sex are remarkably divided, torn as he is between a theoretical commitment to monogamy and a powerful practical attraction to erotic adventuring. The important point, from a conceptual perspective, is that by reducing the gay agenda to the right to marry (and serve in the military), Sullivan effectively abandons the gay movement's historical commitment to sexual expressiveness. In place of the rich and varied sexual cultures that gays have traditionally fostered, he advocates "the idea of homosexuals without sex." If his views prevail, the result will be a drastic impoverishment of gay eroticism.

Warner also dismisses as utopian Sullivan's proposal to limit gay politics to outlawing public discrimination while leaving private citizens free to exercise their prejudices. He rightly sees this conception as deriving from nineteenth-century liberalism, with its laissez-faire fetishism. In his view it wildly underestimates the force and pervasiveness of antigay sentiment. Its practical effect would be to leave untouched "almost the entirety of homophobia and sexism and the countless daily relations of privilege and domination they entail." In other words, Sullivan would eliminate the only kind of gay politics that might actually make a difference. Hence Warner charges that Sullivan's program not only desexualizes gays but depoliticizes them as well, that Sullivan envisions a world in which gays will confine themselves to monogamous romance, foregoing both their traditional eroticism and their adversarial politics.

The intellectual centerpiece of *The Trouble with Normal* is Warner's critique of gay marriage. He argues that marriage is fundamentally "unethical" because it discriminates. In particular it discriminates against "sexual dissidents," whose sense of self and well-being is profoundly linked to nonmonogamous forms of erotic expression: "As long as people marry," he writes, "the state will continue to regulate the sexual lives of those who do not marry. It will continue to refuse to recognize our intimate relations—including cohabiting partnerships—as having the same rights or validity as a married couple. It will criminalize our consensual sex." Indeed, Warner argues that the real purpose of gay marriage is precisely to tame queer sexuality. He cites Sullivan's contention, in *Virtually Normal*, that marriage would encourage monogamy and fidelity and thus "guide homosexuals into more virtuous living." Marriage, in other words, would produce good gays, "the kind who would not challenge the norms of straight culture, who would not flaunt sexuality, and who would not insist on living differently from ordinary folk." The marriage project, in Warner's view, is thus not simply a fair-minded effort to win genuine civic equality for gays. It is, instead, a strategic enterprise to repress queer sexual practices. Marriage, he writes, is "a state-sanctioned program for normalizing gay sexuality."

Warner might seem to be defending promiscuity against romance and relationships. But in fact he rejects the generally accepted view—supported by gay conservatives—that one must choose between the two. Among the greatest contributions of queer culture, he argues, "is the discovery that you can have both: intimacy and casualness;

long-term commitment and sex with strangers; romantic love and perverse pleasure." Even the distinction between intimate and casual relations is misguided, since "the most fleeting sexual encounter *is*, in its way, intimate." Queer culture rejects the notion that sex between strangers is strictly physical, while that between couples is richly emotional. Most important, sex with strangers has a significant communal dimension, sometimes referred to by sex radicals as "the brotherhood of promiscuity." "Contrary to the myth," Warner writes, "what one relishes in loving strangers is not mere anonymity, nor meaningless release. It is the pleasure of belonging to a sexual world, in which one's sexuality finds an answering resonance not just in one other, but in a world of others. Strangers have an ability to represent a world of others in a way that one sustained intimacy cannot, although of course these are not exclusive options in gay and lesbian culture." When gay conservatives champion romance over promiscuity, Warner complains, they mimic the straight world's impoverished notion "that people should be either husbands and wives or (nonsexual) friends." Queers, by contrast, have cultivated a much richer array of relationships: "Between tricks and lovers and exes and friends and fuckbuddies and bar friends and bar friends' tricks and tricks' bar friends and gal pals and companions 'in the life,' queers have an astonishing range of intimacies."

Warner deeply regrets that the national gay organizations have capitulated to the conservatives by making the right to marry (along with the right to serve) the central plank of the gay agenda. Moreover he sees a connection between the increased political attention being paid to marriage and "the growing crackdown on all queerer forms of sexual culture in the United States." He is thinking in particular of Rudolph Giuliani's campaign to close gay sex clubs and bookstores in New York City, which Warner fought against as a founding member of Sex Panic (and which, as we'll see in the next chapter, brought him into sharp conflict with Michelangelo Signorile and Gabriel Rotello). Instead of collaborating in the conservative project to "normalize" gays, he calls on the national organizations to return to their historical mission of defending queer sexual expressiveness in all its splendid variety.

At stake in the defense of queer sexual culture, for Warner, is much more than simple erotic gratification. To be sure, he admits that many gays "have found important pleasures and intimacies in promiscuous sex." But above and beyond these pleasures and intimacies—which of course are not to be despised—queer sexual culture also has a transformative effect on its adepts. Repeatedly in *The Trouble with Normal* Warner invokes what he grandly and vaguely refers to as "the world-making project of queer life." He offers no particulars on what that newly made world will look like. But he clearly believes that sexual liberation brings with it the promise of a transformed society. In other words, he rejects the notion that he is simply defending pleasure, while Sullivan is defending virtue. On the contrary, his case for queer sexual expressiveness is an ethical case, and it is every bit as idealistic as Sullivan's case for gay marriage. Ultimately Warner belongs in the long and noble tradition of sexual utopians, stretching from Charles Fourier to Herbert Marcuse, who identify the release of long-repressed erotic desires as the key to social transformation.

The contrast between Sullivan's and Warner's views is breathtaking. It testifies to the dramatically changed intellectual universe in which homosexuals now find themselves. The two men may share a common sexual orientation, but in every other respect they stand for utterly opposed conceptions of the homosexual predicament and the proper goal of gay politics. Sullivan believes that our world needs only minor legal tinkering—the legalization of gay marriage and the right to serve in the military—to render it an entirely satisfactory place for gays to flourish. In Warner's view such legal tinkering will make an already bad situation only worse, because it will further repress queer sexuality and its "world-making" promise of cultural transformation. Who could have imagined that, a mere three decades after Stonewall, gay intellectuals would be advocating such radically divergent notions of the "gay agenda"?

In contrast to Michael Warner's *The Trouble with Normal*, Richard Goldstein's *The Attack Queers* focuses less on the arguments of gay conservatives than on their style, whose central features, according to Goldstein, are vituperation and personal vilification. His book, one might say, pays them back in kind: it is short on argument and long on insult. There is, however, a substantive point to Goldstein's focus on style. Where Michael Warner views the new gay conservatism as an assault on queer sexuality, Goldstein thinks its primary target is effeminacy and the association of homosexuality with gender non-conformity. The "attack" style of gay conservatives—or "homocons," as Goldstein calls them—is perfectly suited to this target: it is, at bottom, an assertion of aggressive masculinity. Andrew Sullivan's bullying intellectual manner carries the subliminal message that, although homosexual, he is every bit a real man, with all of the familiar manly qualities of character. The link between homosexuality and effeminacy is thus broken at the level of language. Of course, the fact that Goldstein's own book is written in a no less aggressively ad hominem style rather undercuts his identification of that style with unabashed masculinism. "Think of Rush Limbaugh with monster pecs, and you've got Andrew Sullivan" is a representative observation.

Richard Goldstein is a journalist at the *Village Voice*, of which he is also an executive editor. For nearly four decades he has written about politics, culture, and sexuality from a progressive perspective. He identifies himself as a member of "the Stonewall generation" of queer radicals, and his purpose of *The Attack Queers* is to reassert the historical tie between gayness and radicalism. "My main aim," he writes, "is to reach those who aren't aware of the rich connections between radical thought and queer sensibility." To the extent that his book has an argument, it is that the gay movement originated on the left and that it violates its essential character when it abandons its leftist roots. The force of this argument is less than overwhelming, especially for conservatives, who concede that gay liberation began as a radical project but insist that the time has come for the movement to

abandon its infantile leftism and embrace political "maturity." Ironically, Goldstein offers a classically conservative justification for gay
radicalism: gays should be on the left because they have always been
on the left. "Why would gay strivers who aspire above all to be normal
still feel bound to the left?" he asks. "The answer is tradition. Culture has its reasons that self-interest does not know, and our culture
grounds us in progressive values. In some sense, you can't be a queer
humanist and a homocon. The gay right exists, just as Jews for Jesus
do, but it stands apart from the sensibility that marks us as a people."
His reasoning is positively Burkean.

Perhaps the central leftist insight about homosexuals now under
attack by gay conservatives is precisely that they constitute a people—
or, in Harry Hay's classic phrase, "an oppressed minority." When conservatives denounce Gay Pride marches, Goldstein argues, they are
attacking not just particular kinds of behavior but, more fundamentally, the idea that gays form a community, bound together by shared
suffering and aspirations. "Their ultimate ambition," he writes of conservatives, "is to abolish the queer community" and replace it "with a
more individuating model in which the mark of liberation is—to use
the famous homocon phrase—'a place at the table.' " Bruce Bawer's
attack on the idea of a gay sensibility and his corresponding invocation
of "the gay individual" are perhaps the clearest example of the conservative aversion to the idea of community. But Goldstein detects a similar contempt for the idea in a remark of Andrew Sullivan's: "Once we
have won the right to marry, I think we should have a party and close
down the gay movement for good." (The provenance of the remark
is uncertain, as is its exact wording. It appears in Michael Warner's
The Trouble with Normal as "Following legalization of same-sex marriage and a couple of other things, I think we should have a party
and close down the gay rights movement for good." So far as I know,
Sullivan has never repudiated the remark.) For conservatives the idea
of community is a kind of "security blanket" that encourages gays to
wallow in their common oppression, just as it keeps them in ideological lockstep with the left. If gays are ever to overcome their feeling
of victimization and their childish devotion to radical politics, they

will have to "lose their sense of community." For Goldstein, on the other hand, the sense of community is itself even more precious than the freedom and equality it is meant to secure. In his view the fundamental difference between gay conservatives and gay progressives is in fact the value they assign to the community: for progressives it is life-defining, whereas for conservatives it is trumped by individuality.

Goldstein argues that the community has been identified as much by gender nonconformity as by sexual orientation. The centrality of gender was already evident in the thinking and behavior of Harry Hay, the *Urvater* of the idea of community. "Decades before queer theory," writes Goldstein, "Hay was hailing gender variance as a revolutionary force. To look at photos of him bedecked in Western jewelry, and perhaps a skirt, is to glimpse a truly self-made American." (When Hay died in 2002, Andrew Sullivan denounced him as a false prophet, ostensibly because he was a Communist but also, one suspects, because he was a flamer.) As Goldstein observes, gender deviancy precedes sexual orientation in the literal sense that it marks most homosexual children well before puberty. Likewise, the deepest source of homophobia, he argues, is not aversion to same-sex eroticism but fear and hatred of gender-bending. "Trans[sexual] activists," Goldstein reports, "have been saying all along that the way we have sex isn't the real reason we're oppressed; it's the way we present gender." In this analysis, the defense of effeminacy and, more broadly, the critique of gender stand at the historical heart of the gay movement and are as fundamental to its identity as the matter of same-sex desire.

Accordingly, Goldstein sees the deepest impulse behind the new gay conservatism as the repudiation of effeminacy. Conservatives aim above all to separate homosexuality from gender nonconformity and promote a hypermasculine version of queerness. "Masculinism," he writes, "is what holds the conservative movement together." I have argued that this impulse appears stronger in Bruce Bawer than in Andrew Sullivan. But Goldstein suggests that Sullivan understates his masculinist convictions in his published writings and that one must turn to his speeches and blog for evidence of his true feelings about gays who flame. "Readers of his website can attest to Sullivan's revulsion at gay styles that depart from the norms of male presentation," Goldstein asserts, and he cites as an example Sullivan's web account of a visit to the Castro district in San Francisco where, he reported, the streets were "dotted with the usual hairy-backed homos. I saw one hirsute fellow dressed from head to toe in flamingo motifs." Hardly a friendly reference, admittedly, but I'm not sure it rises to the level of "revulsion." Sullivan himself defends the remark as mere "affectionate ribbing." A more clear-cut instance of his unreconstructed ideas about gender is an observation Goldstein quotes from the *Stranger*, a Seattle weekly: "I'm all for the cult of masculinity. . . . Last time I checked, that was a major reason I thought of myself as homosexual. But when hypermasculine men tart themselves about like homecoming queens, the entire concept of masculinity is negated. . . . They're big girls in nipple clamps." The most full-throated celebration of manliness comes from a 2001 speech, "The Emasculation of Gay Politics," sponsored by the *New York Times* and attended by Goldstein, in which Sullivan asserted that the differences between the sexes are "based on deep biological realities that are reflected across all cultures and all times. Therefore, to say I don't have to be masculine is to say I don't have to have two legs and hands. We do. That's who we are. We are natural beings." Remarks of this sort Goldstein refers to as "Sullivan's he-man harangues," which, in Goldstein's view, reveal the depth and violence of his contempt for the unmanly. Perhaps so, but I'm inclined to read them as more principled than visceral. Clearly Sullivan is no great fan of gender-bending. But I don't sense in him the irrational aversion to effeminacy I do in Bruce Bawer. Moreover, I see no reason to believe he would soft-peddle his views about gender in his published writings. He is not generally reluctant to offend.

Goldstein's reliance on unpublished sources to construct his case for Sullivan's masculinism is worrisome because Sullivan has accused him of misquotation. When an excerpt from *The Attack Queers* was adapted in the *Nation*, Sullivan gleefully pointed out that Goldstein had distorted one phrase from *Love Undetectable* to the point that its meaning was exactly reversed. In his article Goldstein wrote:

"Marriage, Sullivan has written, is the only alternative to 'a life of meaningless promiscuity followed by eternal damnation.'" The phrase in fact occurs in Sullivan's critical account of the thinking of Christian conservatives who preach that one should "hate the sin, love the sinner": "So the sexual pathologies which plague homosexuals are not relieved by this formula; they are merely made more poignant, and intense. And it is no mystery why they are. If you teach people that something as deep inside them as their very personality is either a source of unimaginable shame or unmentionable sin, and if you tell them that their only ethical direction is either the suppression of that self in a life of suffering or a life of meaningless promiscuity followed by eternal damnation, then it is perhaps not surprising that their moral and sexual behavior becomes wildly dichotic." Goldstein offered the lame excuse that other writers had wrested the phrase out of context and Sullivan had failed to correct them. But it is difficult to resist the conclusion that his sloppiness was tendentious, and one's confidence in his reliability is accordingly compromised. The incident ended in an exchange of insults and without either party seriously engaging the other's argument, which is typical of the personal and intellectual relations not just between Sullivan and Goldstein but between gay conservatives and gay liberals in general.

At one point in *The Attack Queers* Goldstein asserts that Sullivan is even more hostile to promiscuity than he is to effeminacy. "If there's one thing Sullivan hates more than flaming," he writes, "it's 'the libidinal pathology' of queer life." But in fact Goldstein devotes much less attention to Sullivan's puritanism than to his masculinism. To be precise, he argues that Sullivan has radically changed his sexual views, at first denouncing gay erotic misbehavior (and advocating marriage as a corrective) but then, after Michelangelo Signorile's revelation about his on-line cruising, reversing himself and becoming a defender of promiscuity: "He's hectored gay men for their obsession with 'manic muscle factories,' and railed about their dedication to 'a life of meaningless promiscuity followed by eternal damnation' [the infamous misquotation again]. It took a scandal revealing that he advertises for unsafe sex on the Internet (under the screen name RawMuscleGlutes) to get Sullivan to change his tune. Now he argues that gay men should reclaim promiscuity as part of their masculinity. You'd never know that he broke into belles lettres by advocating same-sex marriage as the only alternative to a life of 'hedonism, loneliness, and deceit.' But consistency is the hobgoblin of small glutes." I wouldn't want to deny Goldstein the pleasure of tweaking Sullivan for his gaffe, but the history of Sullivan's sexual opinions doesn't break down neatly into an early puritanism followed by a conversion to licentiousness. Rather, as I've argued, he has been profoundly ambivalent from the start, drawn equally to the idealized purity of marriage and the raw excitement of sexual adventuring. As in the matter of Sullivan's views about masculinity, Goldstein proves to be a less than reliable guide. He's more interested in scoring points—and making phrases—than in doing justice to his subject.

Like Michael Warner, Goldstein complains bitterly about the prominent voice that Sullivan and other gay conservatives have been accorded in the press, especially the liberal press, where, Goldstein argues, their views are taken to be representative of the gay community while more progressive gay writers are ignored. He cites Sullivan's stint as a columnist for the *New York Times Magazine* and the appearance there of several of his important articles (notably those on the "end" of AIDS and on testosterone) as a particularly egregious example of the gay right takeover of the country's elite media. "It's as if," he charges, "the liberal press had designated a black foe of affirmative action like Ward Connerly as the spokesman for his race." He advances the theory that liberals are airing their lingering homophobia by hiring gay conservatives to make the antigay pronouncements that they no longer feel comfortable making themselves. In other words, he argues that homocons like Sullivan are popular not because of any merit to their arguments or grace in their prose but because they appeal to the barely repressed prejudice of liberals, who find in them a respectable way to give expression to their distaste.

There may well be some truth to this analysis, but it has been rendered moot in Andrew Sullivan's case by his falling out with the

Times, from which, according to Sullivan himself, he was banned by executive editor Howell Raines. In Sullivan's view the banning was a simple matter of ideology: Raines, he alleges, is a hard-line leftist who couldn't tolerate his conservative views. The other side of the story is that Sullivan was fired because he made too many mistakes. Either way, denouncing Raines and his liberal regime at the *Times* became an obsessive preoccupation of Sullivan's. When, in 2003, it was revealed that the black reporter Jayson Blair had regularly fabricated stories in the *Times*, Sullivan was positively thrilled at the evidence of Raines's incompetence and perfidy. "Being banned from writing for the *N.Y. Times* by Howell Raines," he crowed, "feels like a huge compliment." In the event, Goldstein's thesis that liberal guilt is the main reason for the prominence enjoyed by gay conservatives has lost some of its traction. But of course Sullivan's fall from grace at the *Times* may reflect a delayed recognition by its liberal editors that they had been guilty of precisely the genteel homophobia that Goldstein accuses them of.

Richard Goldstein's final verdict on Andrew Sullivan and the other gay conservatives is that they are engaged in a hopeless effort to win acceptance in straight society by jettisoning all the traditionally "offensive" aspects of gay identity other than sexual orientation itself. In their desperate desire to fit in they are prepared to sacrifice the unmanly (and unwomanly), as well as the sexually dissolute. They are, Goldstein argues, very much like assimilated Jews in the nineteenth century, hoping that if they can look and act like gentiles they will be treated as equals. The enterprise is not only unsavory—in that it throws the sissies and the sluts to the wolves—but doomed to failure, because straight society, in Goldstein's view, will never rid itself of homophobia, any more than Christian society rid itself of anti-Semitism: "Just as Jews could never be real Christians no matter how hard they might try, gays will always stand apart in a macho society. . . . Receptive intercourse is inimical to macho, and as long as that's the case, men who take it up the ass or in the mouth will be treated with contempt. . . . We will be penalized for our homosexuality no matter how ably we play the gender game." In other words, no matter how butch or how chaste, Andrew Sullivan will never enjoy the acceptance he so manifestly craves.

In some of his darker moments—as when the Roman Catholic Church contemplated banning homosexuals from the priesthood or when the Republican Party failed to repudiate U.S. Senator Rick Santorum's homophobic remarks—Sullivan himself seems on the verge of succumbing to this gloomy assessment. But his official position is decidedly more upbeat. Prejudice, he insists, can be overcome, and straights can learn to embrace gays in their full humanity. Whether the sissies and the sluts will have to be sold out in the process, as Goldstein suggests, is not entirely clear, but certainly their causes won't enjoy the robust defense they got from the generation of Gay Liberationists. The homosexual preferred by Sullivan and his conservative colleagues is manly, monogamous, and undetectable.

CHAPTER THREE

Michelangelo Signorile and Gabriel Rotello: Sexual Conservatives

In the July 14, 1997, issue of the *Nation*, Michael Warner published an essay, "Media Gays: A New Stone Wall," in which he complained that writing about gay issues in the mainstream press had been taken over by a small group of "neoconservatives." He named five men in particular: Andrew Sullivan, Bruce Bawer, Michelangelo Signorile, Gabriel Rotello, and, from the older generation, Larry Kramer. Michelangelo Signorile objected strenuously to the characterization, not just for himself but also for his friend and sometime collaborator Gabriel Rotello. He cited his longstanding and consistent support of progressive causes, like choice and affirmative action, to substantiate his claim to be a man of the left. His protest was just: on most political issues Signorile espouses liberal Democratic views, including, recently, his opposition to the war in Iraq and to virtually the whole of the Bush agenda. Gabriel Rotello is not so active a journalist as

Signorile, but all evidence suggests that he shares Signorile's political opinions. We also know, from the previous chapter, that Signorile and Andrew Sullivan loathe one another and have been trading insults for at least a decade. What, then, are the grounds for Michael Warner's calling Signorile and Rotello "neoconservatives"? And what, closer to home, is my justification for counting them as prominent representatives of "the new gay right," alongside Sullivan and Bawer?

The simple answer is "sex." In the 1990s, Signorile and Rotello inherited from Larry Kramer and Randy Shilts in the 1980s the task of serving as the most outspoken critics of gay sexual conduct. Signorile's criticism isn't limited to sexual issues in the narrow sense, but all the features of the contemporary "gay scene" to which he objects in his influential book *Life Outside* (1997) emanate from the sexual obsessions that, in his view, are ruining the lives of many gay men. Signorile, in other words, can be fairly described as a sexual conservative. Indeed, despite his progressive politics, he stands decidedly to the right of Andrew Sullivan on sexual issues. It thus makes perfect sense that Michael Warner—for whom sexual issues are ideologically preeminent—should label him a "neoconservative." From my own perspective, sex is one of three axes—beside gender and politics—along which gay conservatism can be charted, and both Signorile and Rotello have espoused sexual views that place them firmly on the conservative end of the spectrum.

There is a second consideration that inclines me to include Signorile among the representatives of "the new gay right." The evolution of his political thinking and activity since the late 1980s, when his professional career as a journalist was launched, is basically a story of deradicalization. He began on the far left of gay politics, as a member of ACT UP who was jailed for participating in a zap against Cardinal Ratzinger when he visited New York City. (Signorile stood up in Saint Peter's, before such dignitaries as Cardinal John O'Connor, Robert Bork, and Mrs. William F. Buckley, Jr., and shouted, 'He is no man of God—he is the Devil!') Then in 1989, with his fellow ACT UP member Gabriel Rotello, he founded the magazine *OutWeek* and became the inventor and foremost adept of the practice of "outing"

closeted homosexuals, for which he was denounced as a crazed radical not only by straights but also by many gays. His first book, *Queer
in America*, is an account of his career as an outer and a vigorous
defense of the practice. When it appeared in 1993 (the same year as
Bruce Bawer's *A Place at the Table*), it was widely abused for its extremism. But in fact the book already found Signorile moving in a
more moderate direction, criticizing his youthful "excesses" even as
he offered a reasoned apology for his assault on the closet. Four years
later, when *Life Outside* appeared, the transformation was complete.
The onetime fire-breathing radical emerged now as a stern critic of
gay sexual misbehavior and a celebrant of those segments of the gay
population who had abandoned the fast lane for more conventional
bourgeois lives. Our gay Robespierre had metamorphosed into a gay
Burke. The trajectory of Signorile's career is a striking instance of the
pervasive shift of gay politics to the right.

The very title *Queer in America* fairly broadcast Signorile's radical proclivities. In the early 1990s "queer" made its bid to displace
"gay" as the label of choice for homosexuals who were not only un-
apologetic about their sexual orientation but happy to be perceived as
cultural and political dissidents. It was a linguistic move modeled on
the way African Americans had displaced "Negro" with "black": one
appropriated the oppressor's term of abuse and wore it as a badge
of pride. Queer Nation (which Signorile cofounded) was the most
notable embodiment of this adversarial impulse. "Queer" was in-
your-face, while "gay" seemed soft and assimilationist. "Queer" im-
plied politics—indeed, confrontational politics—while "gay" was just
a lifestyle. Calling his book *Queer in America* was thus a provocation
intended by Signorile to declare his political colors. (A decade later
it seems evident that the "queer" revolution has failed to carry the
day: "gay" has held its own, and many homosexuals, as well as their
straight sympathizers, continue to find "queer" offensive.)

The fundamental inspiration for outing, as Signorile defends it
in *Queer in America*, was the double standard whereby a person's
heterosexual activities were considered a legitimate subject of journalistic comment while any mention of the person's homosexuality

was strictly taboo. Signorile "smelled homophobia" in this differential practice. "It seemed to me," he writes, "that the American media didn't report about the lives of famous queers because they saw homosexuality as the most disgusting thing imaginable." So outing was conceived of as a means of doing battle with homophobia and its principal enabler, the closet, a battle made all the more urgent by the AIDS crisis, because fear and hatred of homosexuality, Signorile believed, were inhibiting an adequate response to the disease.

In *Queer in America* Signorile qualifies the case for outing in a number of ways, not all of them consistent. Most important, he argues that the practice should be limited to public figures. It is particularly appropriate in the case of public figures engaged in hypocritically antigay behavior, such as Republican congressman Jim Kolbe, who supported the homophobic Defense of Marriage Act (DOMA). The "misconception" that private citizens could have their sexual lives exposed is, Signorile thinks, the main reason so many are opposed to outing. To the objection that sex ought to enjoy the protection of privacy, he responds that outers don't speak about people's sexual behavior, only about their sexual orientation: "Sex is private. But by outing we do not discuss anyone's sex life. We only say they're gay." Sexual orientation, in other words, has no more claim to being private than a person's race or sex, even if it is generally less visible than those other markers of identity. If Signorile were to pursue this line of reasoning to its logical conclusion, he would have to abandon his distinction between public and private figures. Why should the sexual orientation of private citizens be unmentionable when their race or sex is not? Moreover, the proposition that revealing a person's sexual orientation says nothing about his or her sex life is obviously specious. At the very least it tells us what the person *wants* to do and, save in the case of the most severely repressed, what in all likelihood the person has in fact done.

Queer in America recounts Signorile's first outing campaigns in the pages of *OutWeek*. He admits to being embarrassed now by the violence of his attacks, which were distinguished by their tendency to break out into capital letters—the typographical equivalent of a scream. Of the closeted Hollywood mogul David Geffen, for example, he wrote in 1990: "EITHER YOU JOIN US OR WE WILL BEGIN IMMEDIATELY TEARING DOWN EVERY WALL, EXPOSING YOUR HYPOCRISIES. We are on the move, joining forces, arming ourselves for the battle—and we're about to make an assault on the ALMIGHTY CLOSET. . . . GEFFEN, YOU PIG, WE DEMAND THAT YOU IMMEDIATELY STAND UP FOR YOURSELF AND THIS COMMUNITY AND DENOUNCE AND DROP GUNS N' ROSES"—an antigay band Geffen had promoted. Three years later, in the book, Signorile concedes that he was overly angry and given to what he calls "tantrum politics." His excuse is the familiar one that you can't make an omelet without breaking eggs and the times were dire: "As has been true in every revolution, there is always a person or group who kicks things off by doing something brutal. . . . We were under siege at the time, and I was operating with a siege mentality. Friends were dying every week." The language of *Queer in America*, by contrast, is unfailingly reasonable, even measured, and unafflicted by a single hysterical capitalization. The wild man of the earliest exposés has yielded, in a remarkably short time, to the sober defender of outing as a legitimate form of oppositional politics.

After Malcolm Forbes, the most prominent subject of a Signorile outing was the spokesman for the Defense Department during the Persian Gulf War, Pete Williams (who is now a correspondent for NBC). Williams was a particularly inviting target, because he was the chief public defender of the military's antigay policies and thus, from Signorile's perspective, not merely a closet case but a hypocrite as well. Williams's outing occasioned the first major clash between Signorile and Andrew Sullivan. In a *New Republic* column, "Sleeping with the Enemy," Sullivan charged that outing was not a politically neutral tactic whose sole objective was to destroy the closet. Rather, it was practiced by "fringe activists" against anyone who failed to conform to their leftist politics. All the targets of outing, Sullivan asserted, were gays at odds with the radical agenda—a characterization that hardly seems to fit Malcolm Forbes or David Geffen, Signorile's two most prominent victims before Pete Williams. As for Williams himself (who goes unnamed in the column), Sullivan claimed that "there was no proof of his hostility to homosexuals, and some evidence that he may have been doing good." The real reason he was targeted was the left's visceral hatred of the military.

Signorile noted slyly that Pete Williams was a friend of Andrew Sullivan's, a fact that Sullivan failed to disclose in his column. More important, Signorile simply denied Sullivan's claim that outing was politically motivated. While the practice may have originated with "street activists," by the time of the Pete Williams affair it had shed its leftist origins and become a principled method for exposing closeted homosexuals, regardless of their politics. "Contrary to Sullivan's assertions," he writes in *Queer in America*, "journalistic outing is not aimed at gay people who are not following an 'agenda,' but at *public figures* and only when pertinent to a story that may or may not have anything to do with an 'agenda'—liberal or conservative." Sullivan, like most critics of outing, viewed the practice strictly from the perspective of the right to privacy and the violence it did to the painfully ambiguous circumstances of many homosexual lives. Signorile, by contrast, defended it in structural and "journalistic" terms as a precisely calibrated technique for doing battle with the central institution of gay oppression, the closet.

Judged against their subsequent confrontations, especially over barebacking, the disagreement between Signorile and Sullivan about outing seems relatively tame. Indeed, *Queer in America* even contains some boilerplate praise for Sullivan's "enlightened, thought-provoking arguments" about gay issues. In later writings on outing, Signorile also makes that case that Sullivan had softened his opposition to the practice, to the point of going in for a little outing of his own. The main piece of evidence is a 1999 *New York Times Magazine* column in which Sullivan criticizes such public figures as Rosie O'Donnell, Ricky Martin, Donna Shalala, Janet Reno, Donna Brazile, Ed Koch, and Richard Simmons for failing to declare their sexual orientation. While obviously pleased that Sullivan had moved in his direction, Signorile was infuriated by Sullivan's unwillingness to acknowledge his change of opinion or to credit Signorile's labors. By then relations between the two had deteriorated drastically, mainly because they found themselves on opposite sides of the gay sex wars, and Signorile's remarks about Sullivan grew increasingly personal and sarcastic. In a 2001 column, for example, Signorile wrote: "Perhaps we shouldn't expect fairness, let alone admissions of intellectual growth and change of heart, from someone so self-obsessed and seemingly insecure. But maybe we can appeal to Sullivan the avowed Catholic, who defends the Pope and has a shrine in his home. Andrew, from one Catholic schoolboy to another, these are not Christian things that you are going. Get thee to a confessional, pronto!"

Sullivan's "change of heart" was, according to Signorile, entirely typical of the general evolution of thinking about outing, among both gays and the public at large. Indeed, his central contention in *Queer in America* is that outing—so angrily denounced when Signorile first practiced it in the late 1980s—is well on its way to mainstream acceptance. He provides an almost Hegelian explanation for the rise and (eventual) fall of the practice: it was made inevitable by gay oppression, and it will disappear when that oppression ends: "To fight outing at this point is senseless and futile, for, as homosexuality becomes more accepted in our society, outing will become more accepted. The two are inextricably tied: as one advances, the other becomes less of an issue. Outing is a natural process that will eventually make itself obsolete." The effect of this analysis is to transform Signorile himself from a radical troublemaker into the neutral vehicle of an inexorable historical process: he might have looked like a rabble-rouser, but in reality he was merely playing a role made necessary by the forces of social change. In this fashion, he reconstructs himself along essentially conservative lines. *Queer in America* tells the story of his radical origins, to be sure, but it presents the "mature" Signorile of 1993 as the disinterested agent of a political transformation whose time had come.

11

Life Outside is subtitled *The Signorile Report on Gay Men: Sex, Drugs, Muscles, and the Passages of Life.* "Report" is meant to echo the "Kinsey

Report," the popular title that became shorthand for Alfred Kinsey's epochal *Sexual Behavior in the Human Male*, but a more accurate comparison would be the *Hite Report*. Like Shere Hite's book—and in contrast to Kinsey's—*Life Outside* is essentially a highly personal evaluation of the sexual mores of its supposed subjects disguised as a work of sociological observation. No professional sociologist would take it seriously. Signorile's "method" is random in the extreme: "In travels across the country over a two-year period, I casually chatted with or more formally interviewed hundreds of gay men and observed them in various environments. I conducted telephone interviews . . . with many more men . . . . Still more filled out lengthy surveys I designed, which I posted in various places on the Internet. Over six hundred responses came in from every corner of the country and the far reaches of the planet." His sample, in other words, was both small and uncontrolled. Signorile simply ignores the established practices of all serious sex studies—like the 1994 University of Chicago volume, *The Social Organization of Sexuality: Sexual Practices in the United States*—which make heroic efforts to assure that their subjects are representative and that significant variables, such as age and class, are controlled for. In terms of method, *Life Outside* invites comparison with Edmund White's *States of Desire* (1978), which more candidly represents itself as a selective survey of gay male sexual behavior without any pretense to scientific accuracy (and which recounts a story of libidinal extravagance every bit as sympathetic as Signorile's is hostile). The two books tell us more about the sexual ideology of their respective authors than about the worlds they pretend to describe.

Life Outside is a binary book. It is constructed as an invidious comparison between two antithetical gay worlds: the world of the circuit culture, which is promiscuous, body obsessed, and drugged, and the world of "life outside," the folks beyond the city who are leading normal middle-class lives, mostly monogamous, and growing old gracefully. The contrast is supposed to be purely descriptive, but from the start the language is slanted against the circuit partiers and in favor of the "outsiders." At the end of his introduction, Signorile frankly admits his parti pris: "It is my hope, and it is the ambition of this book, that many gay men within the culture of narcissism and hedonism that envelops much of the gay world will follow in the footsteps of a great many others, gay men who have discovered a more rewarding, fuller, and richer life, outside." Narcissism and hedonism are the villains of the piece. Its heroes are the aging gay men who have escaped the urban sexual cesspool.

Signorile contends that the circuit has become a dominant force in the gay world. Its origins go back to the late 1970s and early 1980s, when, he reports, about a thousand men started flying back and forth between New York and Los Angeles to attend parties at places like the Flamingo, the Saint, and the Probe. It grew spectacularly in the 1990s, with the parties now taking place all around the country and even beyond it. By 1996, he estimates, there were fifty parties a year, regularly attended by "tens of thousands" of men. Usually they were staged in resort hotels, such as the Wyndham in Palm Springs, and their denizens spent the weekend dancing, taking drugs, and having sex. Signorile himself attended the White Party at the Wyndham. The hotel's four "sprawling" floors, he tells us, were transformed into "a virtual bathhouse," with men going from room to room, often in groups, to join orgies. (I am a regular visitor to the Wyndham, where I attend a bridge tournament every December. I have trouble wrapping my mind around the idea that its prefabricated rooms, filled with superannuated card players, were only recently the site of a moving orgy.)

Signorile's most immediate objection to the circuit is that it promotes unsafe sex. In particular, he argues that the partiers' excessive drug use lowers their inhibitions and dims their critical faculties. The stimulant of choice, crystal meth, produces the lethal combination of heightened excitement and a deep mental stupor, and in this aroused and dazed condition condoms are often forgotten. Signorile doesn't have actual evidence that the circuit contributes to unsafe sex, but to deny the connection, he says, is "defying . . . commonsense logic," and he invokes the consensus of drug counselors, psychotherapists, and HIV-prevention workers that crystal meth, more than any other drug, promotes "riding bareback." Indeed, Signorile is so persuaded of the connection between drugs and unsafe sex that he seems prepared to recommend an end to drug use altogether. To the mantra that "Drugs are an important part of gay men's lives," he responds, "That may be true as it stands, but if we're not prepared to change that, and if our AIDS agencies are unwilling to at least distance themselves from that drug use, then we must accept that rampant unsafe sex and HIV transmission . . . will continue to be an 'important part of gay men's lives.'" It is another point of disagreement with Andrew Sullivan, who frequently rails against drug laws and the "War on Drugs" on his blog.

Like his friend Gabriel Rotello, Signorile believes that unsafe sex is again on the rise among gay men and that it threatens a renewal of the AIDS catastrophe of the 1980s. In the September 1994 issue of the popular gay magazine *Out*, he dramatized his conviction by publishing an account of his own fall from grace, an account that he reprints in the introduction to *Life Outside*. The story bears more than a passing resemblance to the unprotected sexual encounter Andrew Sullivan describes in *Love Undetectable*: "Last year I spent a couple of grueling weeks on assignment in Hawaii. One night in a Waikiki gay bar I met your classic gay hunk: tall and masculine, with a buzzed haircut, razor sharp cheekbones, a body of granite, and a Texas drawl. I'll make you see God tonight, he promised, trying to coax me to go home with him. It didn't take much for me to realize I needed a religious experience; we went to his place. As usual, one thing quickly led to another. But not as usual, he didn't put on a condom before we had anal sex, and I didn't demand he use one . . . . I'd had a couple of Absolut Citrons. And I made a quick decision—inside of ten seconds—based on heat-of-the-moment rationalizations that at some distance seem absurd: 1) Since he did not put on a condom, he must be negative; 2) He's a Navy petty officer and therefore is a responsible 'good' boy; 3) Since he's in the military he must be tested every six months and would be discharged if positive; 4) He's absolutely perfect—the gay male ideal—and I don't want to do anything to make him blow off the whole night; 5) I'm sure it'll be okay as long as he doesn't come; 6) This is Hawaii, and the AIDS problem can't be like it is in New York; 7) I'll only do it this one time." The story, which generated attention in the national media, doesn't seem to have any obvious connection with the circuit culture that is Signorile's subject in *Life Outside*. He picked up his trick in an ordinary gay bar, and his lapse in judgment was occasioned not by drugs but by drink. Nonetheless he insists that he had fallen victim to what he calls "the scene." His mistake was not simply an isolated individual case of desire overcoming good sense. Rather his mind had been clouded by the malign ideological forces emanating from the circuit. In other words, *Life Outside* maintains that the values and behavior of the circuit influence a much broader circle of gay men than the mere several thousand who actually participate in the weekend parties. Virtually a whole generation, Signorile suggests, has had its self-conception shaped by the partiers. Accordingly, *Life Outside* is concerned less with the circuit itself than with its pervasive cultural effects.

Even if the circuit did not promote unsafe sex, it would remain objectionable to Signorile because of the physical and moral ideals it promulgates. He especially disapproves of its unreconstructed masculinism, or what he calls its "cult of masculinity." The typical circuit partiers, he reports, are deeply hostile to all manifestations of effeminacy. They cultivate a physical style from which any suggestion of androgyny has been banished, and, without a hint of embarrassment, they express their preference for "straight-acting and -appearing" sexual partners. Signorile notes that the circuit marks the second major eruption of masculinism within the gay community. The clone culture of the 1970s represented a similar repudiation of the link between homosexuality and effeminacy. To be sure, the clone embodied a different conception of masculinity: rugged, hirsute, and mature, where the typical circuit devotee is trim, clean-shaven, and youthful. But Signorile nonetheless stresses that both generations "demonized" the effeminate and thus turned their backs on the Gay Liberation's gender radicalism. His argument here is similar to Richard Goldstein's in *The Attack Queers* and marks a decidedly progressive moment in his critique. It also puts him at odds once again with Andrew Sullivan, who, as we've seen, has a high tolerance for masculinism. I have no reason to dispute Signorile's characterization, but I would draw attention to the anomaly that drag performers figure prominently in the entertainment offered on the circuit. Similarly, the relentlessly butch partiers refer to one another as "circuit queens." One suspects that gender-bending has not been entirely abolished even on the circuit.

Although Signorile's criticism of the "cult of masculinity" seems to put him on the side of the angels, even this most progressive feature of his analysis has a reactionary underbelly. He equates the partiers' masculinism with their enthusiasm for promiscuity. More precisely, he finds a link between the cult of masculinity and the bathhouse sex that flourished in the 1970s and made a comeback in the 1990s. "The allure of baths and sex clubs," he writes, "was their hot, 'masculine' sex, as evidenced by the name of one popular New York bathhouse, Man's Country." The baths, he continues, were "a place for macho men to meet macho men, and the effeminately attired [attired?] man or the drag queen was not welcome." He provides no evidence to support this proposition, and it certainly is not confirmed by what I saw of baths in their heyday. But Signorile is so enamored of the idea that he sometimes uses the phrase "cult of masculinity" as a synonym for promiscuity. His defense of effeminacy is thus compromised by his hostility to sex.

The centerpiece of the cult of masculinity is a distinctive physical ideal, which can be seen in the flesh on the circuit: young, hairless, and, above all, muscled (or "cut," in the language of the partiers). Signorile says he has no objection to the ideal in and of itself, only to the rigidity with which it is imposed and the physical and mental agony its pursuit causes, especially among those not destined by nature to be buff. "Even if we've left the scene far behind or if we've never been a part of it at all," he writes, "a highly commercialized gay sexual culture sells a particular physical aesthetic to us and demands that we conform to it—much in the same way that the fashion, film, and beauty industries affect the average American woman." He invokes Naomi Wolf's *The Beauty Myth* in support of this analogy. He also tells many pathetic stories about men who are obsessed with their bodies and in need of constant validation. Those who don't fit the image experience such masochistic self-contempt, he suggests, that they let themselves be screwed without condoms by the fit and the beautiful. The body ideal is marketed by gay publications, which contain "pages and pages of ads promoting huge biceps, cut abs, perfect pecs, and bubble butts." It is also promoted by gay pornography, which emanates from West Coast studios and is populated with muscled and waxed young men who look like they just walked off a California beach. Signorile makes the reasonable argument that this physical ideal is best understood as a reaction against AIDS—an "antidote to ever heightening fears and anxieties about emaciation and death." Because the ideal is promoted so inflexibly, Signorile characterizes it as "body fascism." It is, he concludes, "one of the most detrimental effects of the cult of masculinity in the gay world because it devalues so many men in the eyes of both themselves and their peers."

The cut body so admired by circuit partiers is of course a creation of the gay gym culture that has flourished in the past two decades, and many of Signorile's interlocutors recount the punishing exercise routines they put themselves through in order to enlarge muscles or reduce fat. But he is more worried about the role of drugs, in particular steroids, in this pursuit of bodily perfection. Steroid use among gays began in the early 1990s when doctors started prescribing testosterone as a treatment for AIDS wasting. Many of the beneficiaries developed superb bodies, and soon the drug's cosmetic effects became the chief reason for taking it. Signorile regrets the phenomenon not just because it is another manifestation of "body fascism" but also because he believes the drug has dangerous side effects and can drastically alter behavior, producing "roid rages" and even violence. His distrust of steroids is another important point of disagreement with Andrew Sullivan (aka RawMuscleGlutes), who has famously celebrated the testosterone-enhanced male body and its heightened aggressiveness.

Signorile's protest against the exaggerated insistence on a certain kind of physique, like his critique of masculinism in general, has a progressive air about it. Like Naomi Wolf, he has set himself against a commercialized and often oppressive culture of the body. But one occasionally feels that he is protesting not just against a particular body culture but against something more basic and inexorable, namely, the preeminence of youth and beauty. From the photos on the cover of his books he appears to be both fit and attractive. But I can't escape the impression that there is an element of sour grapes in his unremitting disapproval of the physical ideals pursued—however mindlessly—by many young gay men. At the risk of sounding like a hopeless essentialist, I would suggest that the aristocracy of youth and beauty in the gay world is not entirely a social construct. To be sure, the demand for a very particular physical type (muscled, hairless, etc) is culturally contingent. But it is based on a homoerotic ideal as old as the Greeks. I've learned to distrust the motives of the middle aged when they complain about the young, especially about their appearance and sexual behavior. Even when the complaints are just (as are many of Signorile's), they can't avoid being tinged by envy.

III

One of the central themes of *Life Outside*, as of much of Signorile's subsequent journalism, is that the new hedonism of the circuit parties represents an abandonment of politics. In this respect, he sees gays in the 1990s repeating the error they made in the 1970s, when the political activism of the Stonewall riots and the early Gay Liberation movement gave way to the "selfishness" and "excess" of the bathhouses. "With the police off their backs," he writes, "many [gay men] simply did what men have empowered themselves to do for centuries: they became as sexually adventurous and indulgent as they wanted to be, denying any responsibility for themselves or others in the process." He cites Bell and Weinberg's finding of the mid-1970s that half the gay men in San Francisco reported having had "at least" five hundred different sexual partners. The same pattern can be seen, he argues, in the way the renewed political activism of the late 1980s and early 1990s, represented by ACT UP and Queer Nation, gave way in the mid-1990s to the rise of the circuit. Indeed, he suggests that some of his old comrades-in-arms from ACT UP and Queer Nation had become "fixtures on the circuit": "The cult . . . seemed to absorb the energy that for many men had previously been poured into activism."

Signorile's immediate fear is that this new hedonism will result in a "second wave" of AIDS infections. The circuit partiers, he argues, constitute what Gabriel Rotello calls a "core group," meaning a concentrated number of men who share sexual partners and thereby dramatically increase their chances of contracting the virus. But his disapproval of the sexual practices of the circuit—like his disapproval of the bathhouse patrons of the 1970s—is not inspired solely by the danger of a revived epidemic. Rather, his aversion is as much moral as medical. The sexual realm for Signorile is essentially a domain of egotism and irrationality. The adepts of the circuit, like their bathhouse precursors, are repeatedly described as "indulgent" and "selfish." At the same time he compares their sexual enthusiasm to religion, a term that, as a lapsed Roman Catholic, he deploys with full-throated Voltairean distaste. Like religion, he implies, sex entails an abdication of critical intelligence. Hence his repeated reference to it as a "cult." Politics, by way of contrast, is the domain of selflessness and rationality. Where the sexual enthusiast is driven by impulse and ignores the consequences of his behavior, the political actor exercises his powers of mind to better the lives of his fellow human beings. Sex and religion belong to the childhood of mankind, while politics marks its coming of age

The antithesis between sex and politics—between a mindless obsession with private pleasure and a reasoned commitment to the general good—is deeply rooted in Signorile's personal history, which he recounts in the second chapter of *Queer in America*, "A Queer's Own Story." The central drama of his life, as he tells it, was his conversion from sex to politics. From his early teens, when he started having sex with other Italian boys under the Brooklyn boardwalk, until he joined ACT UP in his late twenties, his life was dominated by sex. The sex was furtive and guilt-ridden, but his appetite was voracious. "I would go for long periods—months—without sex," he writes, "only to gorge out of control at some point." After he came out as an undergraduate at the University of Syracuse, his life quickly assumed the pattern that would dominate it for nearly a decade. "All of my friends were gay," he reports, "and much of my life revolved around exploring my sexuality." Noticeably absent was any interest in gay politics.

After college he continued in this vein as a young reporter and gossip columnist in New York, where he spent the bulk of his leisure time in gay clubs picking up tricks, and where he remained oblivious of politics. "To the people in the clubs in the early and middle eighties," he writes, "gay politicos who identified themselves as 'activists' were boring. They were so *serious*, we would say, and they were wasting their time. We, on the other hand, were *living* the revolution. Or so we thought." He was also oblivious of AIDS and went on having unprotected sex until 1986.

Then, with the suddenness of the classic conversion narrative of a Saint Paul or a Saint Augustine, he joined ACT UP. The brotherhood of promiscuity was displaced by the brotherhood of politics. In 1988 he participated in the group's "action" against the FDA in Washington, D.C., and felt a sense of fulfillment that far surpassed anything he had experienced in his years as a club habitué. "I had a feeling of exhilaration, the kind of feeling I hadn't had since childhood," he recalls. He abandoned his club life and devoted himself to working "day and night" for the cause: "I buried myself in ACT UP." Not that he gave up sex altogether. In fact he had a "sexy and exciting" relationship with a fellow ACT UPer. But the discovery of his identity as an activist involved a massive transfer of intellectual and emotional energies from sex to politics. In subsequent writing he would recommend just such a transfer to those who continued to wallow in the sexual wasteland of his youth. Contemplating the revelers at the Palm Springs White Party, he writes, "I'm struck by the thought of how, if even half of this party energy could be put toward political action, gay men would be light-years ahead of where they are."

Strikingly ignored in this analysis is any sense that sex itself might be the subject of politics. Yet there is a long and rich tradition of sex radicalism that argues just that proposition. Indeed, the Gay Liberation movement might legitimately be described as a political endeavor to defend a distinct kind of eroticism. Certainly the founders of Sex

Panic, like Michael Warner, believe they are engaged in a political action to protect their sexual way of life. In their view, politics in support of sexual expression is every bit as altruistic and rational as the struggle for democracy or economic justice. In effect, they reject the assumption that sex is a selfish indulgence unworthy of being elevated to a political cause.

Signorile is a bit like a reformed drunk. Having entered the monastery of politics (to adopt his own religious metaphor), he regards his years of sexual adventuring as a sort of binge. In *Life Outside* he protests, "I . . . greatly enjoy sex." But the very fact that he feels the need to make such a declaration betrays his awareness of the book's antierotic animus. Although he seldom sounds so prudish as Bruce Bawer or so condemnatory as his mentor Larry Kramer, his treatment of sex is consistently belittling and patronizing. He is a deeply political animal, and he has achieved a degree of satisfaction as an activist and journalist that obviously eluded him in his days as a club boy. Moreover, much of his political advocacy merits admiration. But one can still regret that he has achieved his political success by denigrating sex.

IV

In part 2 of *Life Outside* Signorile turns to the other half of his binary construction: gay men who are largely untouched by the circuit and its values and who find themselves ever more engaged in the ordinary routines of American life. Perhaps the main reason they are immune to the charms of the circuit, he suggests, is that they have abandoned the cities—the historic centers of gay culture—and taken up residence in the suburbs, where the siren song of the bars and sex clubs is barely audible. These refugees from the gay ghetto are joined by a growing number of out gays who have never left their hometowns, for the simple reason that the greater acceptance of homosexuality in the country has made such an exodus unnecessary. Signorile acknowledges that this "deurbanization" or "deghettoization" of gay life was made possible by the political and cultural labors of the generation of gays who flocked to the cities in the 1960s and 1970s. But its effect has been to repudiate the style of sexual abandon those city dwellers cultivated. The story of "life outside" is one of assimilation and mainstreaming. "Many of these men," he reports, "express needs and desires in life that are just as simple and traditional as the heterosexual people they grew up with: In interviews and surveys, many of these men said their main priority was to meet someone, fall in love, and settle down."

Signorile does not draw an extreme contrast between libidinal urbanites and prudish outsiders. The gay men who have moved to the suburbs (or never left the heartland) are neither particularly moralistic nor conservative. They still share much of the culture of their urban counterparts. They read gay literature, watch gay movies (and gay porn), and, he insists, "espouse a generally sex-positive viewpoint and a rather progressive political perspective." Nevertheless, a major theme in their lives is a retreat from the intense preoccupation with sex that virtually defines the world of the circuit. One of his informants, Adrian, is a classic instance of the reformed sybarite: "I sowed my oats back in the late 1960s and 1970s, and to be very frank I have very little sex. . . . In ten years, I've probably had sex three or four times. It's just taken the back burner. Now, at forty-two, . . . there are other things that are important to me." Most of Signorile's outsiders have more robust sex lives than Adrian. But for nearly all of them sex has suffered a substantial demotion.

An important difference between the city dwellers and the outsiders is their attitude toward fidelity. Signorile sees them pursuing two distinct patterns of coupling: "open relationships" in the ghetto, and what he calls "postmodern monogamy" in the suburbs. An open relationship is one in which the partners are emotionally committed to each other—"emotionally monogamous," as they put it—but don't expect sexual exclusivity. Moreover, to avoid the resentment and jealousy that plague heterosexual couples, they are supposed to discuss their sexual adventures and even share partners.

Open relationships received an imprimatur of sorts from David McWhirter and Andrew Mattison's 1984 study *The Male Couple: How Relationships Develop*, which examined 156 gay couples in San Diego over a five-year period (after Stonewall but before AIDS) and found that none of them was monogamous. McWhirter and Mattison also reported that some couples felt their philandering "contributed to the stability and longevity of their relationships." Signorile complains that the study was based on an unrepresentative sample and has been used by sex radicals for "political" purposes, namely, to argue that monogamy is an unnatural condition for gays. He also complains that gay men who happen to be in faithful relationships have been made to feel embarrassed by their conformity to "heterosexual" standards. Worse yet, some on the sexual left have even "pathologized" gay monogamy. In reality, he argues, the notion that gays are naturally nonmonogamous is a construction of the Stonewall generation, which held that gay men were uniquely equipped to do battle with our culture's long history of sexual repression. Gays, in other words, were destined to bury monogamy.

The "postmodern monogamy" that, according to Signorile, prevails outside the ghetto differs from traditional monogamy in acknowledging the possibility, even the inevitability, of occasional lapses from fidelity. In this respect it concedes that gay men, just because they are men, will never attain the degree of exclusiveness that straight couples aspire to in theory and sometimes achieve in practice. But the straying should be limited, and it should be kept secret. Where candor is the necessary cement of an open relationship, postmodern monogamy demands discretion. "These men," Signorile writes, "accept that either they or their partner might have sex outside the relationship, perhaps while on a business trip or while the other is away from home, but that, unless such outside sex becomes too frequent, it is not a problem, and that acknowledging and discussing these activities might do more harm than good." To the generation that made the sexual revolution, hypocrisy of this sort was the ultimate sexual sin. But for the practitioners of postmodern monogamy it is a reasonable price to pay for keeping their relationships afloat.

Signorile doesn't expressly take sides in this argument between open relationships and postmodern monogamy (nor does he reveal his own practice). But he leaves the firm impression that postmodern monogamy is the wave of the future, while open relationships are a historical relic, left over from the heady days of Gay Liberation. He is also clearly skeptical of the claim that opening up a relationship contributes to its durability. In effect, he won't acknowledge that sexual boredom is a genuine problem and that efforts to deal with it are more than exercises in self-delusion. Nor does he have anything to say about the growing practice among some gay couples of taking a third (and younger) person into the relationship, which is the subject of William Mann's 1997 novel *The Men from the Boys* and represents an interesting attempt to introduce sexual variety while avoiding the dangers—to both body and soul—of open relationships. More generally, he appears to share none of Michael Warner's fear that the turn to monogamy—even of the more forgiving, "postmodern" variety—means a pathetic impoverishment of the sexual expressiveness of traditional gay culture.

Among the foremost benefits of the "deurbanization" of homosexuality, in Signorile's view, is a more tractable attitude toward aging among gay men. In particular, he applauds "the death of the lonely old queen," the notion that the inevitable price of a youth devoted to sexual indulgence is an old age of bitter regret about the pleasures one can no longer obtain. Because the old queen remains fixated on youthful bodies and faces, he experiences his own physical deterioration as especially hateful. One old queen confessed to Signorile, "I think I'm, well, quite honestly, *grotesque*."

But while old queens really exist, Signorile insists they are a dwindling lot, especially in the suburban gay culture that, he argues, is in ascendancy. He cites Raymond Berger's study *Gay and Gray: The Older Homosexual Man* to support his contention that older gay men are no more likely to be alone or isolated than young gay men. More to the point, he insists that they do not inhabit an erotic desert. Rather, most of them have "active sex lives" with which they are largely satisfied, and, in contrast to the stereotype of the lonely old queen, they actually prefer men "within their age range."

I hope I will be forgiven if I express skepticism about these "findings." I don't doubt that most aging gay men muster the dignity to accept the sexual implications of their diminishing powers and attractions. But that does not mean they rejoice in their constrained circumstances or stop fantasizing about the young and the beautiful. The vast market in gay pornography, which of course is populated by hunky bodies and sold mainly to older customers, suggests otherwise. Signorile thinks he is doing battle with outmoded and repressive ideas about sexual attraction when he debunks the circuit's obsession with youth and beauty while championing the suppler attitude toward aging of his outsiders. Indeed, he suggests that the stereotype of the lonely old queen has been kept alive by malignant doctrines emanating from the circuit and its cult of masculinity. "The cult of masculinity cannot survive," he asserts, "without keeping the stereotype of the lonely old queen alive." No doubt youth can be fetishized and old age demonized, but the sexual preeminence of the young is finally more than a cultural plot. One need not be an evolutionary psychologist to believe that it is grounded in nature and even has a Darwinian logic to it. What is wanted is the grace to accept the sexual privileges of youth and the wisdom to abandon those privileges when the time comes, without using aging as an excuse to malign the young for being sexually attracted to the young.

Signorile believes that the stereotype of the lonely old queen is being undermined by a new familiarity between young and old gays, especially outside the ghetto. He notes a growing interest among older gays in mentoring the young, and points in particular to the role of academics. One of his informants tells him, "Most of the older gay men I know, who are my good friends, are university professors and teachers." Having been in this position myself, I recognize the phenomenon, but I would caution against thinking that these cross-generational relationships seriously compete with the romantic or even intellectual interest of the young in one another. Signorile apparently expects that the adult mentors will be able to steer their charges away from the errors—especially the sexual errors—of their predecessors. "We must create a generation of mentors," he writes, "not simply to offer to those men who are growing older a sense of meaning and purpose in their lives beyond the cult, but so that younger men will interact with older men outside of the bars, nightclubs, and other sexual venues. We must begin the process of passing down the truth to young gay men so that they don't make the same mistakes, so that they learn from the rest of us about the emptiness of the cult." You get the feeling he hopes to talk the young out of their obsession with sex. It is neither a realistic nor, in my view, a desirable goal. No amount of mentoring, I'm happy to believe, will persuade the young to forgo their pursuit of sexual bliss, even when that pursuit risks foolishness and brutality. But the hope is an accurate reflection of Signorile's antierotic bias.

v

Signorile would reject my charge that he is hostile to sex. He firmly believes that his reservations about the sexual behavior of some gay men are inspired solely by his concern that the behavior is physically dangerous. The "excesses" of the circuit and the ghetto stand condemned not because they offend traditional notions of restraint but because they are causing a rise in HIV infections and threaten a full-scale return of the epidemic. He shares this analysis with his friend Gabriel Rotello, from whose book *Sexual Ecology: AIDS and the Destiny of Gay Men* he draws much of his argument and evidence. But I am convinced that his hostility to the circuit is "over-determined," in Freud's sense of the word. That is, while fears about AIDS might be sufficient to explain that hostility, it is no less inspired by his belief that the sexual practices of the circuit are also morally regrettable: they damage the psyche as well as the body. In general, he does not state his moral objections forthrightly, for fear of sounding judgmental. He is more comfortable presenting his case as an argument against disease. But he is betrayed by his text's freighted language and invidious oppositions—between "inside" and "outside," between the ghetto and the heartland, between crazed circuit queens and sober suburbanites. In ways both subtle and direct, the reader of *Life Outside* is left in no doubt that he is being urged to choose not just health over sickness but long-term contentment over fleeting pleasure.

The fusion of medical fact and moral judgment—of reportage and editorial—in *Life Outside* follows the example set in the 1980s by Signorile's two great ideological forebears, Larry Kramer and Randy Shilts. Larry Kramer's anger about the way gay men were killing themselves expressed itself in language of fierce sexual disgust. In his epochal *New York Native* piece of March 1983, "1,112 and Counting," he asked of his fellow gay men, "How can they value life so little and cocks and ass so much?" The same judgmental tone pervades Randy Shilts's monumental history of the early years of the epidemic, *And the Band Played On*, most witheringly in its account of the airline steward Gaetan Dugas, so-called "Patient Zero," on whose cross-country erotic adventures Shilts blamed the early spread of the disease. Signorile's moralism is less overt than Kramer's or Shilts's, but it is cut from the same cloth. The titles of two of his important AIDS essays, "641,086 and Counting" (1998) and "And the Band Played On II" (1902), pay obvious tribute to his mentors. In *Life Outside* he frankly acknowledges his debt to Kramer, who, for his part, has called *Queer in America* "one of the most important books of the twentieth century." The intellectual lineage is unmistakable.

I do not mean to imply that Signorile's concerns about AIDS are inauthentic—a medical veneer to disguise the moral objections he lacks the courage to express directly. On the contrary, he is genuinely exercised by the prospect of a revived epidemic. Moreover, AIDS is a central preoccupation of *Life Outside* and of much of his subsequent journalism as well. In all his writings on AIDS, the main target of his criticism, whether named or not, is Andrew Sullivan, whom he appears to consider the single most important source of misinformation about the disease. We are confronted with the intriguing paradox that Sullivan, who is HIV-positive and a political conservative, takes the more benign view of the epidemic, while Signorile, HIV-negative and a liberal, fears the worst. Sullivan is, in effect, a defender of pleasure against Signorile's insistence that pleasure must be curtailed for the sake of health.

Signorile offers a jaundiced analysis of "the protease moment," the introduction in the mid-1990s of the new combination drug therapies that Andrew Sullivan hailed in his *New York Times Magazine* essay as marking the "end" of the epidemic. Signorile does not deny that the new drugs have dramatically reduced the mortality rate and restored many sufferers to health. But he denounces the idea, propagated by Sullivan, that protease inhibitors have transformed AIDS from a death sentence into a "manageable" condition. He notes that the "excruciating" drug regimen fails in many cases, and even when it works it can have "deformative" side effects. But his main worry is that the drugs are encouraging gay men to indulge in sexual behavior that guarantees a repeat of the tragedy of the 1980s. "I predict a replay of what happened over 15 years ago when AIDS first surfaced," he warns. Because of the "hype" that "it's not so bad to get HIV," safer sex practices are being abandoned. The likely consequence is that the virus will mutate into new drug-resistant forms that can fatally reinfect HIV-positives and spread to HIV-negatives as well. He cites a 2001 study from the Centers for Disease Control and Prevention showing that infection rates among young gay men have doubled since 1997 to argue that a second epidemic is in fact already upon us. One would almost think he believes we were better off before protease inhibitors. Then, at least, the fear of death forced gay men to curb their appetites and held the disease at a steady, even declining, level. The new pharmaceutical dispensation, by contrast, threatens another conflagration.

Andrew Sullivan of course believes that protease inhibitors not only saved his own life but woke the gay community from its long nightmare. He dismisses Signorile's dire predictions as alarmist. On his blog he has repeatedly noted that the second epidemic has failed to materialized and that, in the most recent studies, infection rates have fallen once again. Signorile's apocalyptic pronouncements, he suggests, betray a deep-seated puritanism.

Signorile and Sullivan have had their angriest confrontation over the issue of "barebacking," the conscious decision to have anal intercourse without condoms. The practice emerged into prominence in the mid-1990s. At first, apparently, it was confined to HIV-positive men, who argued that because both parties already had the virus no harm could result. But according to Signorile it has since spread to

HIV-negatives, especially on the circuit. He blames this development on protease inhibitors and the notion that AIDS has become "a very manageable disease." But he condemns the practice even among positives, because, he says, it risks "reinfection" with different strains of HIV, some of which might prove to be resistant to the new drugs. In "The 'Bareback' Lie" he invokes findings presented at the 2002 International AIDS Conference to support his conclusion that bareback sex "may be fueling the epidemic among gay men in the United States and promoting the transmission of drug-resistant strains of HIV."

Signorile considers Sullivan among the most influential apologist for barebacking. He points to the lyric account, in *Love Undetectable*, of his condomless anal intercourse with an old friend, an episode that Sullivan celebrates as an almost magical release from the epidemic's years of repression and guilt. Even more damning was Sullivan's internet advertisement for bareback sex, which of course Signorile was the first to reveal and which led to the donnybrook I described in the last chapter. At the time, Sullivan rejected the argument about reinfection as "weak and hypothetical." The reaction was consistent with his skepticism about the claim that AIDS is once again on the rise. But he has since been forced to concede that reinfection is "absolutely possible." He still defends the raw encounter described in *Love Undetectable*. "It was," he writes, "part of my psychological and emotional healing process—to return to the sexuality that HIV had stigmatized and to celebrate it once again." But he admits that even HIV-positive men should "rethink what we are doing and why."

I am not qualified to judge the argument over reinfection or to settle the question of whether a new eruption of the epidemic threatens. As far as I can tell, the evidence is inconclusive. But I am struck that Signorile and Sullivan come down so decisively on opposite sides, with Signorile calling Sullivan an "AIDS denier" while Sullivan obviously considers Signorile a "sex denier." It is hard to avoid the conclusion that their disagreement is more ideological than empirical. Sullivan is determined to think well of sex. It is for him a profound human experience in whose absence life is radically impoverished, indeed not even fully human. He is inclined to suspect those who caution about its dangers of harboring puritanical impulses. For Signorile sex has no such existential significance. It is more like a pleasant diversion. Only the self-indulgent would refuse to rein it in, even eliminate it altogether, if there is reason to think it poses a threat to life and limb. That the two should arrive at opposite conclusions about matters like barebacking and reinfection is, one feels, all but preordained.

VI

Life Outside both charts and applauds the deradicalization of gay life. True, the most vivid and controversial feature of the book is its account of the circuit, which Signorile sees as a menace to the community's physical and mental well-being. But the bigger story is how more and more gays are embracing the values and routines of the American mainstream—integrating themselves into the economy, rejoining churches, cultivating ties with their biological families, and, not least, tempering their sexual conduct. Appropriately, Signorile's title inscribes that bigger story. It is of course a conservative story, fundamentally indistinguishable from the story Bruce Bawer tells in *A Place at the Table*.

Gabriel Rotello's *Sexual Ecology*, which appeared in the same year —1997—as *Life Outside*, delivers a similar message. Significantly, the two books received a joint review from the historian of science Daniel Kevles in the *New York Times Book Review*. Rotello's subject is the behavior that he believes brought us the AIDS epidemic and that he fears promises a repetition of the catastrophe. Rotello and Signorile are of course long-standing friends who worked together in the late 1980s and early 1990s, first as members of ACT UP and then as founding editors of *OutWeek*. Not surprisingly, they share many views, and their careers have followed a similar trajectory. Both have abandoned their early radicalism to write cautionary tales urging gay men to moderate their behavior. Their books are nevertheless quite different in tone and character. *Life Outside* is a colorful and somewhat ramshackle work of popular sociology, based largely on the author's personal observations. *Sexual Ecology*, by contrast, is a closely reasoned and systematic analysis of the AIDS epidemic, drawing on the conceptual resources of epidemiological theory and written in calm, measured prose. Where Signorile is garrulous and combative, Rotello is subdued and cerebral. One is surprised to learn that before he became an AIDS activist Rotello was a rock musician, an identity that might seem a better fit for Signorile.

Rotello's central theme in *Sexual Ecology* is that the AIDS epidemic was caused by what he calls "anal multipartnerism"—an appropriately ugly neologism for so deadly a practice. The epidemic was not, as Jeffrey Weeks has asserted, a "historic accident" but the predictable result of changes in the sexual behavior of gay men. The first change was that anal intercourse became much more common—indeed, became the defining act of gay male sexuality. All authorities agree that anal intercourse is the main avenue by which the virus was spread. But by itself, Rotello argues, the increased popularity of anal intercourse was not sufficient to cause an epidemic. For that to occur another item had to be added to the equation: multipartnerism, that is, having sex with a large number of partners, which of course happened on a massive scale, at least in urban centers like New York and San Francisco in the 1970s.

The final—and most controversial—element in Rotello's analysis is the proposition that this anal multipartnerism flourished in what he calls "core groups." The idea is that the HIV virus grew to epidemic force within a delimited group of gay men who had multiple anal encounters *mainly with one another*, thereby creating a "biological feedback loop" that "amplified" the disease. Had these men confined their sexual activity strictly to other members of the core, all of them would have become infected and died, but the "epidemic" would have remained relatively modest in scope. But "core group" theory assumes that members of the core also have sex (if less often) with individuals outside the core, who serve as a "bridge" to the gay population at large.

The importance of core groups was suggested to Rotello by the work of Rice University statistician James Thompson, who developed a theoretical model illustrating mathematically the dramatic increase in infections one could expect from such concentrated behavior:

"Thompson created two scenarios. In one, a theoretical gay population has a uniform sexual rate of 30 contacts per month. In the other,
the total number of contacts within the population remains the same,
but most sexual activity is shifted to the core, so that 10 percent of the
population has 150 contacts per month and the other 90 percent has
only a few contacts. Thompson showed that despite the fact that this
second population has the same total number of contacts as the first,
the fact that most of the contacts have been shifted to the core has the
same effect as if the entire group had doubled its number of contacts.
In other words, the same number of contacts produces twice as much
new infection if those contacts are concentrated among a small core
of men." "Core groups," in short, spectacularly increase the rate of
infection, pushing the disease over the epidemiological threshold.
According to this analysis, AIDS grew to epidemic proportions because of the sexual practices of a limited but concentrated number of
individuals.

The phrase "anal multipartnerism" might seem to imply that anal
intercourse and having a large number of sexual partners bear an
equal burden of responsibility for the epidemic. But the logic of Rotello's analysis forces him to assign much greater importance to multipartnerism. It alone explains why the disease has not spread to
heterosexuals. The vagina is nearly as congenial an environment for
the virus as the rectum. Admittedly, the rectum may be "somewhat
more susceptible to infection" than the vagina, but the difference,
Rotello insists, is "nowhere near sufficient to account for the several-
thousand-fold difference in HIV prevalence between gay men and
comparable heterosexuals in the developed world." The important
difference between gays and straights, in other words, is not that
gays have anal intercourse while straights have vaginal intercourse
but that gays (or a core group of them) have sex with a categorically
greater number of partners. The existence of AIDS in the third world,
especially in Africa, also points to multipartnerism (and core groups)
as the key factor. The African epidemic, for instance, is sustained by
a prostitute population that has sex with itinerant workers. Similarly,
the epidemic among intravenous drug users is sustained by addicts

who share needles, which enables the virus to achieve the degree of concentration that rises to epidemic levels. Once again we have the essential ingredients of multiple acts among a delimited, or "core," population.

Rotello sketches a history of gay male sexual behavior in the twentieth century to support his contention that that behavior changed dramatically in the decades immediately before the epidemic. His starting point is George Chauncey's important study *Gay New York*, whose main finding is that homosexual sex took a remarkably different form in the early decades of the century. Typically it occurred not between gay men but between straight men (known as "trade") and gay men (known as "fairies"), with the latter fellating—or, less often, masturbating—the former. AIDS, Rotello argues, could never have flourished in this "fairy culture," not only because anal intercourse played no significant role but also because it provided little opportunity for a venereal virus to circulate or achieve epidemic concentration. Even when anal intercourse occurred, the virus could not be passed on, because a "fairy" was always on the receiving end. In effect, the fatal "loop" couldn't materialize

"In the middle of the twentieth century," Rotello states, this system was displaced by what he calls "modern gay sexual culture." In terms of its susceptibility to a venereal epidemic, the crucial difference in the new culture was that gay men now sought out other gay men (rather than straights) for sex, and the strict separation between active and passive roles gave way to "versatility," meaning that the men alternately played both insertive and receptive parts. The necessary preconditions for the epidemic, one might say, had been established. But Rotello argues that at midcentury anal sex was still the exception rather than the rule, and the number of sexual partners remained limited, at least by later standards. The essential core groups that could support an epidemic hadn't yet come into existence.

The really crucial changes happened in the 1960s and 1970s, when anal intercourse moved from the periphery to the center of gay sexual culture and multipartnerism skyrocketed. Rotello attributes both of these developments not to the unfettering of some natural desire for

anal sex and multiple partners but to specific ideological forces emanating from the sexual revolution and Gay Liberation. "Multipartner
anal sex was encouraged, celebrated, considered a central component
of liberation," he writes. He cites several examples of the way the practices were promoted by gay authorities and ideologues. But far more
critical than any of these ideological factors, in Rotello's view, was a
single—and fatal—institutional development: the rise of the baths.
The first modern bathhouses emerged in the 1950s and 1960s. In
the 1970s their numbers increased spectacularly: by the end of the
decade there were more than two hundred major baths in the country, generating $100 million a year in business. In the same decade
almost all baths installed orgy rooms or mazes. It has been estimated,
Rotello reports, that 15,000 men visited the baths every weekend in
San Francisco, and each of them could have sex with "a dozen or more
partners in a single visit." He also argues that "these huge numbers
imply that many of the men who frequented the baths were repeat
customers." That is, they constituted precisely the sort of core group—
men who had sex mainly with one another—that made the epidemic
possible. And, in fact, AIDS first appeared among gay men who had
very large numbers of partners: according to interviews conducted
by the Centers for Disease Control and Prevention, "the first several
hundred gay men with the disease had an *average* of 1,100 lifetime
partners."

Some defenders of the baths have argued that, had these institutions not existed, the same amount of partner swapping would have
taken place elsewhere—in parks, alleys, or private homes. But Rotello
insists that the baths "maximized sexual partnering and sexual mix-
ing in a way no other institution could possibly match." It is a strong
claim but, it seems to me, an unassailable one. The baths, with their
large number of virtually naked customers packed into a confined
(and comfortable) space, were uniquely efficient in promoting multiple sexual encounters. If, as Rotello contends, anal multipartnerism
is indeed the key to the epidemic, one cannot even imagine a more
lethal arrangement.

Sexual Ecology is as much a work of prescription as analysis. Its argument that AIDS was a product of multipartner anal sex among a core group of men provides the basis for Rotello's views about what needs to be done both to contain the current epidemic and to prevent its repetition. Without doubt the most controversial conclusion to which his analysis leads him is that we cannot rely on condoms as our sole defense. He takes a dim view of the so-called "condom code"— the belief, which became orthodoxy in the 1980s, that the epidemic could be ended simply by persuading gay men always to use a condom when they had sex. In his cynical analysis, the condom code—or "safer sex"—was devised as a way to reduce HIV transmission while preserving intact "the multipartnerist ethic of the gay sexual revolution." He derides it as "a classic 'technological fix,'" which diverted attention from the broader "ecological" factors that supported the epidemic. "By declaring that condoms fulfilled all obligations to prevention," he writes, "the culture of multipartnerism could be justified and celebrated anew. . . . Gay men could return to the golden age of the sexual revolution that had started to fade into memory during the dark early days of the epidemic." He admits that if everyone actually did use a condom every time, the epidemic would indeed end. But he clearly regards that prospect as utopian. Not only do condoms fail in about 10 percent of cases, but "no more than about half of all gay men have ever used condoms consistently as a response to AIDS." He also denies that condoms should get credit for the decline in new infections at the end of the 1980s. Rather, the cause was "saturation": virtually nobody was left to infect. The conclusion seems inescapable: "If it is impossible to contain AIDS solely with technology by getting everyone to use condoms every single time they have sex—and it appears that it is—then we need to create a sexual ecosystem that 'forgives' such occasional lapses."

What would be the elements of such an "ecosystem"? The most obvious is that the sort of promiscuity advocated by Gay Liberation will have to give way to a much more restrained style of sexual partnering. The ideal solution, Rotello implies, would be monogamy. In the early days of the epidemic, before the condom code became established, there was a brief moment when some AIDS authorities urged "partner reduction" as a way of combating the disease. Rotello clearly considers the failure of that proposal—which was denounced as homophobic— a tragic missed opportunity. Indeed, he regrets that no one "followed the partner reduction theory to its logical conclusion and endorsed monogamy as a form of prevention, working to create and shore up institutions that supported long-term monogamous gay relationships and attacking the ethic of multipartnerism." But he is reluctant to embrace monogamy without qualification, perhaps because he fears sounding moralistic, but more likely because he regards it as impracticable. Instead, he makes the more modest proposal that monogamy be recognized as a legitimate choice, not dismissed as a repressive imitation of heterosexuality. "One of the basic ways to make gay culture more sustainable," he writes, "is to create an honored place for relationships and fidelity. By this I mean that we need to encourage a new gay ideal that validates and supports relationships rather than one that validates and honors sexual adventurism, sexual consumerism, and risk taking."

More realistic than strict monogamy, he suggests, is the sort of serial monogamy supposedly practiced by lesbians: "What is needed is a self-sustaining culture in which people feel socially supported *within their identities as gay men* to settle down with individual partners for significant periods of time." The "lesbian model" provides the desired protection against disease while making allowances for sexual boredom. It would result in "a culture that is safe but not smothering, that still leaves open the possibility of sexual freedom while respecting relationships and encouraging fidelity." Whatever the merits of this idea, it has provoked the anger of some lesbian intellectuals. When Rotello published a synopsis of his argument in the *Nation*, Carolyn Dinshaw and Margaret Long wrote in to protest his assumption that "there's a single homogeneous community of happy serially monogamous dykes out there—one that's ready (as always) to show men what they need to know."

While sympathetic to fidelity, Rotello is eager to demonstrate that he is a flexible monogamist. Hence his support for the practice, pioneered in Australia, known as "negotiated safety," which is a complex agreement between partners of the same HIV status allowing for sex outside the relationship while keeping the risk of viral transmission "to negligible levels." The agreement calls for regular HIV tests and permits unprotected anal intercourse after three months without infection. Most important, it authorizes "extramarital" sex only on the most precise and rigorous terms. The crucial stipulation reads: "If you're HIV negative, discuss and promise each other that you will avoid anal sex outside the relationship, or that if you or your partner fucks anyone else, condoms will be used." Rotello praises negotiated safety as "a deep ecology approach to AIDS prevention." The judgment seems surprising when one considers that it is really a variation on the condom code and countenances sexual adventuring, which, after all, is a mild form of multipartnerism.

The first requirement, then, for what Rotello calls a "sustainable gay culture" is that the "brotherhood of promiscuity" give way to a new respect for long-term relationships, which, while not always strictly monogamous, would approach the conditions of monogamy. To avoid a recurrence of the epidemic, extreme multipartnerism must be abandoned. But what about anal intercourse, which, in Rotello's analysis, represents the second fatal term in the equation that produced AIDS? He is not so bold—or so foolhardy—as to propose that it too must go. But he clearly thinks it has been oversold, and he wouldn't mind if it fell into disfavor. Indeed, one of his complaints against the condom code is that it is geared to promote anal intercourse, when in fact the prudent thing would be to avoid the practice altogether: "The code implicitly and even explicitly encourages gay men to engage in the riskiest sexual practice of all: anal sex . . . . The central slogan of prevention has been to 'use a condom *every* time,' implying that anal sex is what all gay men do *every* time. In attempting to make such messages alluring, gay prevention literature has frequently emphasized how 'hot' anal sex is. Posters depict beautiful young men holding condoms and exhorting each other to DO IT!, reminding themselves that SAFE SEX (read: anal sex) is HOT SEX. No one knows how strongly these messages have influenced young gay men to believe that anal sex is the kind of sex they ought to have, but it would not be surprising if they were very influential." The hint of contempt in this passage suggests that anal sex, far from being what gay men naturally desire, has been promoted by ideologues. One suspects that Rotello himself doesn't particularly enjoy it, even though he says in his introduction that he was once "an enthusiastic participant" in the sexual culture he now criticizes. Certainly he shows no sympathy for the contention of sex radicals that anal intercourse is central to the meaning of their lives—that asking them to give it up is like asking heterosexuals to give up vaginal intercourse. Here it appears instead as a kind of historical accident, perhaps even promoted by AIDS advertising, and not the necessary or logical centerpiece of gay male sexuality.

One might expect that, having raised doubts about anal sex, Rotello would be an advocate of the so-called "oral substitution" strategy, which urges gay men to have unprotected oral sex on the theory that it will keep them from having anal sex. But in fact he has raised a red flag about oral sex, first in a long article in *Out* magazine and then again in his book. "There is evidence," he writes, "that receptive oral sex—sucking—while significantly less risky than receptive anal sex, nonetheless carries a risk of HIV infection." Authorities put that risk at between one-tenth and one-fifth the risk from anal sex, but Rotello thinks it may be greater. "Oral sex," he concludes, "holds a risk that is significantly higher than many gay men would feel comfortable with." Like anal sex, it is more dangerous when practiced with multiple partners, which, Rotello argues, is precisely what happened in the new sex clubs that opened in the late 1980s and flourished in the 1990s. Moreover, it is simply not the case, he insists, that more oral sex means less anal sex. In reality, the two go hand in hand. He also raises doubts about the safety of deep kissing, which he says is a vehicle for transmitting infections such as hepatitis, herpes, and mononucleosis.

So an "ecological" approach to gay male sexuality would embrace monogamy—at least of the serial variety—and shun anal intercourse, unprotected fellatio, and perhaps even deep kissing. What, then, one might ask, are two boys to do? Rotello's answer is that they should return to the sexual practices of the ancient Greeks. Citing the scholarship of Michel Foucault and David Halperin (though hardly in their spirit), he notes approvingly that Greek men limited their sexual activity to "a single mode of copulation," namely, "intercrural" intercourse, or intercourse between the thighs. "No glory holes or fisting orgies for them, no psychological musings on the 'meaning of semen exchange' in homosexual relations," he comments sarcastically. "With no apparent evidence of homosexually transmitted epidemics looming before them," he continues, "the Greeks nonetheless seem to have practiced a form of 'safer sex' almost identical to the one that modern gay men need to adopt: moderation within the relationship, and few or no outside partners." He fails to note that Greek pederasty was as much an educational as a sexual institution and that it was age-specific and temporally limited: adolescents entered into the relationship with an older mentor but were expected to become husbands and fathers as adults. As David Halperin has cogently argued, the relationship was not really homosexual in the modern sense ("There were no gay men in ancient Greece," Halperin writes), so it is hardly surprising that it found a different physical expression. Obviously Rotello doesn't propose that gay men should literally go back to Plato and limit themselves to intercural intercourse. But he does envision a drastic reduction in their sexual repertoire. For him, the primary significance of the Greek example is that it shows homosexual desire is sufficiently malleable to undergo the transformation he is urging. The sexual culture that brought us AIDS was historically contingent and can be replaced by a much healthier culture. "Far from being the universal default mode of male homosexuality," he writes, "the lifestyle of American gay men in the seventies and eighties appears unique in history. . . . Gay male sexual behavior has changed many times. No one can say that implacable biology ordains failure, that gay social organization is fixed, promiscuous, and doomed." Rotello's emphasis on the malleability and historical contingency of homosexual desire aligns him conceptually with the social constructionists. But where social constructionists generally find themselves on the radical side of the sex wars, Rotello is unusual, perhaps unique, in deploying constructionism to conservative ends.

Central to Rotello's "ecological" point of view is the conviction that the behavioral changes he calls for must be permanent, not merely a temporary strategy to be abandoned once the epidemic has passed. He pictures us living in a viral jungle, with countless bugs out there just waiting for the opportunity to promote themselves. The AIDS virus, he argues, had been around for decades, perhaps "even centuries," when the bathhouse revolution provided it with an ecological niche in which to flourish. The opulent history of sexually transmitted diseases supplies this bleak vision with an aura of plausibility. Of course one might argue that no previous venereal disease was as lethal as AIDS, and thus there is no reason to assume that any of the viruses in waiting will also be so deadly. More likely they will merely be annoying or mildly inconveniencing. In this sense, one could still maintain that AIDS was an accident after all. But Rotello takes the grim view that we should act as if our lives are at stake. Because anal multipartnerism enabled one deadly virus to achieve epidemic dimensions, prudence demands that we assume it can do so again. Hence his demand that the ethic of sexual restraint he advocates be permanent.

Rather mysteriously, toward the end of *Sexual Ecology* Rotello seems to reverse himself and hold out the prospect, however distant, of a world rid of deadly viruses. Science, he says, may one day learn how to destroy such viruses, and, he adds, "When the last microbe is tamed, when the problem of mutation is solved, people will be free to decide how to behave based on ethical and social considerations, not epidemiological ones." It would mean that gay men could choose to take up anal multipartnerism once again without risking catastrophe. "When that day dawns it will be up to that generation to decide how to behave, and they may just decide that such behaviors, being without biological harm, are justifiable, moral, and rewarding. Someone may then pick up the yellowed pages of this book and wonder what all the fuss was about." The rather wistful tone of the passage suggests that he doesn't look on that prospect with much enthusiasm, and the concession doesn't fundamentally disturb the book's astringent view of our biological predicament.

VIII

I argued in the case of Michelangelo Signorile that his criticism of gay sexual behavior, while ostensibly inspired by the danger such behavior poses to health, is as much moral as medical. Moreover, it is the moral element in his critique that inclines me to call him a sexual conservative. Is the same true of Gabriel Rotello? Is he too at bottom a moralist who has constructed an elaborate scientific argument to disguise what are basically ethical objections to gay sexual culture? A number of sex radicals, like Michael Warner and Walt Odets, have made just that accusation. In a gentler vein, the historian Martin Duberman, reviewing *Sexual Ecology* in the *Nation*, admits that Rotello's scientific argument is compelling but suspects that moral convictions lie beneath its biological veneer. Rotello doesn't "overtly preach the inherent superiority of monogamy and lifetime pair-bonding," Duberman writes, "yet that seems to be where his heart is." The suspicion that Rotello is a moralist must remain just that: a suspicion. Unlike Signorile, who wears his convictions on his sleeve, Rotello carefully avoids translating his case into moral terms. "Let me simply say at the outset," he begins, "that what I describe below are biological, not moral, events." At the express level, *Sexual Ecology* is in fact remarkably consistent in advancing its case along biological rather than moral lines. Its sole grounds for criticizing particular forms of behavior—like anal multipartnerism—are that they pose a risk to physical well-being, indeed to life, not that they are immoral or even psychologically damaging. In this respect Rotello is fiercely single-minded. His argument is a model of consistency.

Yet the suspicion persists. Like Martin Duberman, I too can't escape the feeling that the book's scientific case is underwritten by a moral vision—indeed, by the very same conservative moral vision that informs Signorile's book. The main evidence is rhetorical: Rotello's language is frequently overwrought. It implies that the behavior he describes is not merely unhealthy but bad. The most obvious example is his habit of referring to conduct he disapproves of as "extremist." At least since Barry Goldwater's 1964 presidential campaign—in which the candidate proclaimed that "Extremism in the defense of liberty is no vice"—the word has carried a substantial moral freight. Thus one senses more than a hint of disapproval when Rotello speaks of "a culture of unprecedented sexual extremism" and "the full resurgence of gay sexual extremism" or when he complains of "those who are living at the most extreme fringes of gay sexual life" and "the extremes of the gay fast lane." A similar tendentiousness is on display when a newspaper is said to "trumpet" (rather than merely assert) the virtues of promiscuity or when advocates of sexual expressiveness are called not simply "sex-positive radicals" but "self-proclaimed sex-positive radicals." Admittedly, the gestures are small, and one could hardly build a federal case on them. But they contribute subtly to the impression that Rotello's judgments are indeed morally inflected. Or perhaps we should return to Freud's notion of overdetermination: while Rotello's argument is manifestly driven by his biological concerns, that doesn't mean it is uninfluenced by his moral convictions.

I of course have an interest in finding Rotello guilty of moralism. It serves to advance my case that, like Signorile, he too is a sexual conservative. But in the end I can't persuade myself that he is a Savonarola merely posing as a disinterested scientific observer. On the contrary, I am convinced that his analysis is inspired by an entirely genuine belief that gays risk another holocaust if they return to the sexual culture of the 1970s. My conviction derives not just from the extraordinary rigor and cogency of his argument in *Sexual Ecology* but also from the autobiographical revelations in a recent on-line essay, "What I Know Now about Fear." The essay recalls the profound impact on Rotello of the death from AIDS of his lover—his "soul mate," he calls him—and of "half" of his friends. He was seized by the "fear that all of my friends would die, that our world would end, and that we would disappear."

It is precisely the fear of death—of universal gay death—that looms over the pages of *Sexual Ecology*. One may take issue with the book's argument (as do the figures to whom I will turn presently), but to suggest that its grim vision is somehow inauthentic—a scientific fantasy concealing a deep puritanism—is gratuitous.

Among the sex radicals who have challenged the argument of *Sexual Ecology*, Michael Warner has been the most outspoken. Gabriel Rotello is even more hateful to Warner than is Andrew Sullivan. A major reason for his animus is that he and Rotello came into direct conflict over the Giuliani administration's effort to regulate New York City's sex clubs. In his *New York Newsday* column, Rotello urged Giuliani to enforce the state health code that prohibits oral, anal, or vaginal sex in commercial spaces. The recommendation was consistent with the logic of his analysis in *Sexual Ecology*, where he writes, "Core group behavior has traditionally been facilitated by commercial sex establishments, and reducing such behavior necessarily involves regulating such establishments, either by the gay community itself or by health authorities." Michael Warner, by contrast, is a founding member of Sex Panic, which came into existence expressly to combat Giuliani's crackdown on sex clubs. Rotello, in Warner's view, has been sleeping with the enemy. Worse, he has been a major inspiration for the enemy's hostile acts.

Warner categorically believes that the only way to control AIDS and end the epidemic is to practice safer sex: that is, to work toward universal condom use. Anything that calls the condom code into question—like Rotello's argument in *Sexual Ecology*—actually helps to sustain the epidemic, because it invites carelessness and despair. The same is true of any "moralistic" assault on traditional gay sexual practices, like anal intercourse and promiscuity: it serves only to increase the shame gays feel about their sexuality, leading them to give up on protecting themselves or even to rebel against prevention. Warner regards the "barebacking" phenomenon as just such a rebellion.

Warner rejects outright the argument that sex clubs are causing a rise in AIDS infections. On the contrary, he insists that such public venues, because they promote the use of condoms, actually help keep the epidemic in check. "Not a single study has shown that a new wave of infections can be traced to sex clubs," he writes. "Most risk happens in the bedroom, not the backroom." Unfortunately, he has no evidence to support this assertion, which is counterintuitive and ignores the case Rotello mounts that the multipartnerism encouraged by baths and sex clubs dramatically increases the likelihood of infection.

Warner is particularly contemptuous of Rotello's idea that the AIDS epidemic was caused by the sexual behavior of "core groups," namely, the adepts of the bathhouse culture of the 1970s. He says flatly that the idea is unproven—and hence, by inference, that it is a fiction inspired by Rotello's puritanism. He does not engage with the reasoning—such as the use of James Thompson's mathematical model—through which Rotello supports the idea. He makes no allowance for the fact the core group theory, like any causal theory, is advanced on the grounds of its high probability and its superiority to rival hypotheses, not because the evidence for it is airtight. Of course Warner's objection to the idea is entirely understandable: it makes the sort of sexual behavior to which he is devoted and for which he claims "world-making" powers the chief villain in the AIDS tragedy.

The disagreement between Rotello and Warner is not fundamentally about AIDS prevention. To be sure, as we've just seen, Warner contends that Rotello's prescriptions will worsen the epidemic. But his argument is thin and slapdash and can't compete with the carefully reasoned case Rotello mounts in *Sexual Ecology*. The real clash between the two is (to put it grandly but correctly) about the meaning of life. For Rotello the basic good he seeks to preserve is physical survival. If our sexual practices can be reasonably shown to risk death, they must be abandoned. For Warner the basic good at stake is sexual pleasure and the spiritual and social transformation it promises. The threat of death haunts Rotello and determines his sexual views, while for Warner a life without the promise of bliss is no life at all. It is another instance of Freud's epic battle between Eros and Thanatos.

IX

Perhaps the most interesting counterpoint to the sexual conservatism of Michelangelo Signorile and Gabriel Rotello has come from Eric Rofes, an AIDS activist and sex radical who served as executive director of Los Angeles's Gay and Lesbian Center and of San Francisco's Shanti Project. Rofes calls himself "a proud, promiscuous homosexual." In *Reviving the Tribe: Regenerating Gay Men's Sexuality and Culture in an Ongoing Epidemic* (1996) and *Dry Bones Breathe: Gay Men Creating Post-AIDS Identities and Cultures* (1998), he offers a radically different way of thinking about the epidemic and a vigorous defense of traditional gay sexual culture. His starting point, ironically, is a conviction he shares with Andrew Sullivan, namely, that the AIDS crisis is over. He does not mean that the disease has been conquered but simply that it no longer dominates the lives and imaginations of gay men as it did from the mid-1980s to the mid-1990s. Both medically and psychologically we have entered the post-AIDS era. "The tremendous weight of loss has eased and the terror within has abated," he writes.

Rofes differs from Sullivan in insisting that the end of the AIDS crisis cannot be attributed solely to protease inhibitors. Rather, the post-AIDS era was already underway before the new drugs came on the scene in 1996. He finds evidence of this changed outlook in the sexual cultures that began to emerge earlier in the decade, especially the opening of new sex clubs in New York, San Francisco, and Los Angeles. He also points to the very developments that Michelangelo Signorile and Gabriel Rotello bemoan, notably, the rise of the circuit and the sudden popularity of sexual practices, like barebacking, that had been proscribed during the height of the epidemic. Protease inhibitors certainly assisted in this renaissance of gay sexuality, but Rofes thinks a more fundamental factor was the sheer determination of the community not to give up the forms of pleasure and sociability that had defined the gay revolution from the beginning. Gay men, he suggests, refused to be defeated by the epidemic. After fighting back in the heroic prevention efforts of the 1980s, they were not about to let the disease rob them of their sexual birthright. The "tribe," in short, has "revived."

Rofes is not surprised that the revival has provoked a backlash. It differs from previous sexual panics in being spearheaded not by the usual suspects but by gay journalists, with Signorile and Rotello at the head of the pack. The key to understanding figures like Signorile and Rotello, Rofes argues, is to remember that they are men now approaching middle age who condemn the young for doing the very things they themselves did when they were young. "Rather than address their own misgivings about aging, ageism, and the gay cultures they inhabited in the 1970s and 1980s," he writes, they are "transferring a powder keg of fears, disappointments, guilt, and rage onto young gay men and their emerging post-AIDS cultures." They represent a failure not just of empathy but of the ability to master their own envy and resentment. What Rofes hears in their writings is "a long, sad, middle-aged whine."

He is especially critical of Signorile, whom he accuses of "stereotyping" and "scapegoating" the young gay men on the circuit. Signorile's practice in *Life Outside*, according to Rofes, is to seize on extreme cases and treat them as if they were representative, without bothering to argue the case. He focuses on "men obsessed with their pecs, addicted to a life of steroids, and never satisfied with their size, but there is no evidence that these men are typical of those who participate in the life of the circuit." Similarly, the partygoers are abstracted from the fabric of their lives and reduced to a series of reprehensible sexual practices: "They become men without jobs, families, meaningful friendships, or cultural or political concerns." At the same time, they are unfairly made out to be the main source of the continuing epidemic—the new "core group," "the contaminating other." He contrasts Signorile's exaggerated and decontexualized treatment of the circuit with the more nuanced analysis of Lynette Lewis and Michael Ross in *A Select Body: The Gay Dance Party Subculture and the HIV/AIDS Pandemic* (1995), which is based on interviews with a fuller cross-section of participants and offers "a rich portrait of a complicated social structure" without the reductive and moralistic conclusions of *Life Outside*.

Rofes charges that the same rigid moralism distorts Signorile's discussion of "barebacking," whose profound psychological motives he refuses even to consider. "For many men," writes Rofes, "an important part of anal sex is semen exchange—receiving another man's semen in the butt or ejaculating one's semen into another man—and the use of condoms alters the meaning of the act in a way that is not always acceptable." He adds: "I will not judge these men harshly." It is a point of view he shares with the AIDS psychologist Walt Odets, whose book *In the Shadow of the Epidemic: Being HIV-Negative in the Age of AIDS* (1995) accuses AIDS authorities of lying when they tell gay men that condoms won't interfere with the pleasure and meaningfulness of their lovemaking. Rofes himself continues to avoid unprotected anal intercourse, but he clearly considers the decision to have raw sex a legitimate choice, in which one must balance the interests of health against those of pleasure and meaning. Not surprisingly, he is a fan of "negotiated safety," which strikes just such a balance.

Rofes has less to say about Gabriel Rotello. He argues that the analysis of the AIDS epidemic in *Sexual Ecology* is "wrong" and regrets that the book has been used "to fuel repressive actions that undermine public health," by which he means the shutting down of sex clubs where safer sex is encouraged. He complains that Rotello's notion of science is old-fashioned and positivistic, without sufficient appreciation that "all science [is] impure and loaded with biases." But his main objection to *Sexual Ecology* is that it supplies ammunition to the enemy. "I was horrified," he writes, "to watch the Sunday morning television show *This Week* . . . and hear former Education Secretary William Bennett throw Rotello's book in the face of HRC Executive Director Elizabeth Birch. . . . Bennett assailed Birch and other gay leaders for refusing to acknowledge and criticize the promiscuity of gay men and hold them responsible for the continuing AIDS epidemic." Rofes's critique, like Michael Warner's, is weakened by his failure to take on the book's central argument about the importance of anal multipartnerism in the epidemic. He merely asserts that "Rotello's discussion of the role of the 'core groups' in 'sexual ecosystems' lays the groundwork for the kind of scapegoating that emerges in moral panics." The charge is undoubtedly true (as Rotello himself acknowledges), but it doesn't affect the correctness of his analysis. It is one thing to say that a book lends itself to misuse, another to say that it is in error.

Whether or not Rotello's analysis of the causes of the epidemic is correct, Rofes is certain that his prescription for ending it and preventing a recurrence is misguided. In effect, Rotello seeks to scare gays into modifying their sexual behavior by telling them they risk disaster. But, counters Rofes, "decades of public health research show that tactics of guilt, fear, and repression exacerbate public health crises rather than deter them." I suspect that the reality is more complex—that fear is an effective deterrent for some but counterproductive for others. The truth is that Rofes seems prepared to accept a certain level of infection as the price that must be paid for the preservation of gay sexual culture. "Contrary to the views of Gabriel Rotello," he writes, "we believe that we are already making progress in bringing down the level of infection among gay men, and we are not panicked by the realization that, absent a vaccine, this is likely to take many decades."

Rofes's deepest commitment is to sexual liberation, which, he contends, is "inextricably bound" not only with gay liberation but with the women's movement and "the emancipation of youth." Sexual expressiveness is so integral to the meaning of gay men's lives that they are prepared to risk even life itself: "We value the enactment of our desires and will not always give them up in a grand gesture of sacrifice to the epidemic. We may understand, in the value system of middle-class America, a long life and safety are supposed to be motivation enough to throw a cold blanket over our smoldering desires, but many gay men will not give up meaningful sexual acts uncritically and forever." We are back again to the bedrock conflict between a commitment to life and a commitment to meaningful pleasure. Rofes hopes the two can be reconciled, but if forced to choose, one senses he would opt for pleasure. He is unwilling to sacrifice what he views to be his fundamental identity, even for the sake of survival.

In Michelangelo Signorile's view, Eric Rofes, like Andrew Sullivan, is simply a victim of "AIDS denial." Rofes's case is particularly galling because he was once "a sane voice in HIV prevention." Signorile dismisses *Dry Bones Breath* as "one of the nuttiest books about the epidemic to emerge this year" and expresses relief that it received little attention, and what reviews it did get were "quite critical." That characterization hardly fits George de Stefano's laudatory notice in the *Nation*, in which de Stefano calls Rofes the Antonio Gramsci of the gay movement. "A longtime sex radical," Signorile writes, "Rofes can't seem to bear the idea that, in order to end the epidemic, gay sexual culture must go through some major changes. So he's decided we must simply accept the amount of HIV infection that we are experiencing and stop viewing AIDS as a 'crisis.' In other words, get used to it." The assertion is not entirely unfair, but it ignores Rofes argument about the deep significance of sexual expression to many gay men's sense of self. Sex for Signorile is rather like a good meal: one is happy to have it, but it requires no grand sacrifice to give it up if you learn it has been poisoned. For Rofes, by contrast, sex is a central existential experience that we must be prepared to defend even when it poses a threat to life.

X

I feel I shouldn't end without trying to clarify my ambivalence about Signorile and Rotello and the sort of sexual conservatism they represent. I truly am of two minds about them, and while I can't reconcile the contradiction, I can at least spell out the opposed lines of thinking that are the sources of my dilemma. Like Martin Duberman, I am fundamentally persuaded by the argument, advanced by Rotello and supported by Signorile, that the sexual culture of the 1970s, above all, the anal multipartnerism of the baths, was the cause of the AIDS epidemic. The related contention that a revival of that sexual culture, such as began to take place in the 1990s (albeit on a more modest scale), threatens a recurrence of the tragedy is necessarily more speculative, but it strikes me as a reasonable extrapolation from the experience of the 1970s. Thus I am not inclined to dismiss Rotello and Signorile simply as "sex-negative" or "self-hating" moralizers. Rather, I believe their thinking is inspired by a genuine fear of death and a plausible conviction that death is the price we will pay if we don't change our sexual ways. This view might be described as conservative in the profoundest philosophical sense. It accepts that we live in a vale of tears and that nature is utterly indifferent to human happiness—that life, as the man said, is nasty, brutish, and short. Sexual desire is nature's trick to facilitate reproduction, and it is hedged about with danger. To be sure, the human imagination can make sexual pleasure an end in itself, divorced from any reproductive function, but nature has no interest in such a project. On the contrary, the long history of venereal disease—at least one of which we know is deadly—suggests there might well be a Darwinian logic at work to limit sex to its necessary biological task. From this perspective the contention of sex radicals that we can pursue our bliss seems naïve and utopian. It betrays a lack of that sense of prudence that conservatives have always recommended as the way to survive in an indifferent—indeed a hostile—universe.

When I examine my own sexual practice over the years of the epidemic, it seems to have been guided by this pessimistic line of reasoning. Once I became aware that the disease was sexually transmitted, I had no trouble convincing myself that the only sensible thing to do was to get out of the sex business, at least of the sort I had bought into during the 1970s. In effect, I embraced the conservative logic later urged on gays by Rotello and Signorile: sex was great, but it was clearly dispensable when faced with the prospect of death. Of course (and here we come to the other side of the argument), I was in my forties when the epidemic hit, and it was no great sacrifice for me to change my ways. In fact, I had already done so before word of the disease began to leak out: at the end of the '70s I had settled into a monogamous relationship more suited to my declining charms. So while I embraced the conservative view that values life over pleasure, it was a suspiciously easy choice. Had I been in my twenties, I wonder if I would have made the same choice. Perhaps, but it certainly would have been much harder—a genuine choice, and not simply the more or less inevitable withdrawal into relative chastity that comes with age.

On the other hand, I think it is impossible to underestimate the force and pervasiveness of American puritanism, of which homophobia is simply a branch. Anyone who listens to cable news or pays attention to the best-seller list knows that we are awash in moralizers, or what Dan Savage calls "virtuecrats." In such a culture one has reason to be suspicious of writers like Signorile and Rotello who recommend a sexual code that, from a practical point of view, is indistinguishable from that preached by the William Bennetts and Robert Borks of the world. To be sure, Signorile and Rotello are inspired by an entirely secular concern for life and health, not by antique religious prejudice. But one worries that they have not thought enough about the reactionary uses to which their ideas lend themselves. More radically, one suspects that, unconsciously, their thinking has been influenced by the deep strain of sexual repression that is their American birthright—that they are conservatives not just in the deep philosophical sense (for which I have some sympathy) but in the superficial moralistic fashion of right-wing pundits and religious fundamentalists. Precisely this suspicion has provoked me to give their critics, like Michael Warner and Eric Rofes, a sympathetic hearing. Warner and Rofes are right to complain not just that Rotello and Signorile offer comfort to the enemy but that they are unwitting accomplices in our culture's age-old war against pleasure.

So I remain divided between, on the one hand, the recognition that we sometimes have to constrain our dangerous desires and, on the other, an abiding hostility to America's antierotic prejudice. In my prudent moments I'm inclined to accept Rotello's and Signorile's gloomy analysis and embrace the wisdom of restraint. But in my radical moments—which are admittedly somewhat attenuated these days—I want to protest their implication in our culture's long history of repression.

EPILOGUE: *QUEER AS FOLK*

During the time I have worked on this book I have found myself compulsively watching the Showtime cable series *Queer as Folk*. The program, which is about a group of gay friends living in Pittsburgh, debuted in the fall of 2000. Although it got mixed reviews, it quickly found a large audience—among gays, obviously, but increasingly among straights as well, especially women. It is based on a British series of the same name, but where the British show ran for nine episodes, there have already been fifty-four episodes of the American version, with a fourth season still to come. Whatever the show's artistic merits, it constitutes, I'm persuaded, a cultural watershed, above all because of its frank depiction of gay sexuality—which had been so spectacularly missing from such earlier gay-themed shows as *Ellen* and *Will and Grace*. The very first episode contains a long, believable, and explicit (though not yet pornographic) scene of anal intercourse.

To be sure, *Queer as Folk* is on cable television, which enjoys greater latitude than network television. But the show's dedication to presenting the reality of gay sex on a mainstream outlet nonetheless marks a quantum leap in gay visibility. I can't imagine that its impact on the consciousness of gays—who are finally seeing the central fact of their lives portrayed on television—has not been significant, and I suspect it has had a no less considerable effect on its straight viewers, for whom gays are now not just rights-bearing citizens but desiring bodies.

While I was originally intrigued by *Queer as Folk* as a cultural phenomenon, I have increasingly found myself watching it as a kind of foil to the conception of gay life advanced by the conservative intellectuals I treat in this book. Not that the show expressly addresses gay conservatism. None of the characters is a conservative, and indeed the phenomenon goes entirely unmentioned. But the show engages all the issues about which gay conservatives are exercised, and it offers what might be called a counter-vision to the conservatives' ideas about what is good and what is bad in gay culture. Bruce Bawer, I suspect, would dismiss it as the ideological brainchild of aging and ever more irrelevant liberationists. But the program's large audience and staying power suggest that it presents a picture of gay life with which many identify. I don't want to make the unsustainable claim that *Queer as Folk* shows us a representative slice of today's gay world. It suffers from the distortions one finds in any television drama: the characters are too attractive, the situations too melodramatic, the dialogue too contrived. But even with its conventional exaggerations, it captures many important elements of contemporary gay reality.

The show's central theme, if I may put it somewhat grandly, is the dialectic of sex and romance, of lust and love. The four friends, who are in their late twenties and early thirties, have sex on the brain and spend all their evenings, it would seem, cruising for tricks. They do so mostly at a dance bar and sex club called Babylon, where at least one scene in virtually every episode is set. Babylon is the story's sexual center of gravity. With its go-go boys, strobe lights, thunderous music, uniformly young and muscled clientele, and active backroom, it might be thought of as Pittsburgh's little piece of the circuit world decried by Michelangelo Signorile in *Life Outside*.

At the same time, the friends—with one significant exception—are also looking for love. They hope that one of the tricks they go home with will turn out to be a permanent mate. Their search is more than usually exigent because they are at a delicate age and fear they will soon no longer be competitive in Babylon's Darwinian world of the young and the beautiful. They suffer from an intense age-consciousness, which is the source of many cutting remarks and makes thirtieth birthdays (two are "celebrated" during the series) a source of high anxiety.

The character who copes least well with this predicament is an accountant named Ted. He is at a serious disadvantage: not only is he slightly older (thirty-three when the series starts) but he is also relatively plain. Yet his desires are as imposing as anyone's. He's addicted to pornography and jokes desperately about how many men have rejected him every evening. He enters into a series of disastrous relationships, first with a drug-addled twink, next with a fellow opera queen, who seems an appropriate soul mate but whose flabby body and bad breath turn him off, and then with a young man he meets at a gay church, who can't deal with the discovery that Ted by this time has become a pornography entrepreneur with his own Web site and a stable of performers. He eventually settles into an uneasy relationship with another of the friends, Emmett. The two are genuinely fond of one another and sexually compatible, but an underlying dissatisfaction drives Ted to drug addiction and a catastrophic swing on the circuit.

Ted's opposite, in a sense, is Michael, who works as a clerk (and later manager) in a store resembling Wal-Mart. He has a crush on his high school friend Brian (to whom we'll come in a moment) but nonetheless manages to make a successful transition to long-term relationships. During the first season he moves in with a chiropractor, who is a little older but still fit and attractive, and in the second season he pairs up with a handsome gay studies professor nearer his own age. Nevertheless he continues to visit Babylon with his friends, if now more as an observer. Even for this most romantically conventional of the characters, the show declines to set up a sharp antithesis between the world of relationships and the world of sexual adventure—between Signorile's "life outside" and "life inside."

The third friend, Emmett, is a queen with a big heart. Naturally he is the object of much teasing by his straight-acting pals, but the show takes a highly indulgent view of his effeminacy, which he embraces with utter comfort. True, at one point he says of himself, "I'm a big nelly bottom who wishes he were a beefy, brutal top." But the remark is a bit of self-deprecating humor, and in fact he fully identifies with the queenly tradition. He is, in short, Bruce Bawer's nightmare. Perhaps because he is both a little younger and quite desirable, he is less obsessed about finding a partner. In one of the first season's most amusing episodes, he promises God to give up sex if he turns out to be HIV-negative. He then falls into the clutches of an exgay group, and we are presented with the hilarious prospect of a flamer trying to go straight. But he is soon back alongside his friends in Babylon. Ironically, he turns out to be the best relationship material of them all, taking up first with a much older man (who dies of a heart attack while screwing him in an airplane toilet), and then, as noted, settling down with Ted, where he proves by far the more satisfactory partner.

The exception is Brian, a glamorous, stylish, and successful advertising executive who is at once admired, envied, and (often) loathed by the other three. He is a relentless cocksman and principled antiromantic. Love, he says, is for lesbians and benighted straights. At one point he admits that he has sex with between twenty and thirty different men a month. The show maintains a brilliantly ambivalent attitude toward his unbridled hedonism and sovereign indifference to the opinion of the world. On the one hand, we are invited to see him as damaged goods, a man whose narcissism and brittleness are defense mechanisms against the hurt of an uncaring father and a homophobic mother. On the other, he is presented as someone who has completely liberated himself from the repressive conventions of heterosexuality and whose utter contempt for straight society makes him the ultimate gay hero. Significantly, he serves as the model for a comic book superhero created by two of his friends: "Rage, Gay Crusader, cold-hearted ad exec by day, defender of queers by night." And, indeed, while he loves to denounce do-gooders, he is repeatedly shown to be secretly working for the welfare of his friends and the gay community at large.

In the series opener Brian picks up a beautiful seventeen-year old boy, Justin, and takes him home to bed (resulting in that revolutionary scene of anal intercourse I mentioned at the outset). The seduction poses what will prove to be the central question uniting all the episodes: what is to become of Brian and Justin? Almost immediately we develop the expectation—perhaps the hope—that this teenager, who has fallen in love with Brian on the first night, will ultimately bring our Lothario to heel—that Brian, the principled antiromantic, will lose his heart to the boy and give up his wicked ways. That expectation provides the show with its overarching dramatic structure. But the expectation is never fulfilled, at least not in its conventional form. True, Brian does become attached to Justin and continues to have torrid sex with him (thereby violating his rule that he never does it with anyone more than once). Indeed, they gradually drift into something resembling a relationship. But Brian refuses to tell Justin that he loves him, and he refuses to be jealous. More important, he continues to have sex with other men (on what appears to be an unreduced schedule) and does so often right in front of Justin himself. Brian is an equal opportunity philanderer: for his nineteenth birthday he buys Justin a hustler. By the end of the second season Justin despairs of taming his man and goes off to live with a boy his own age, but he returns midway through the following season. In the meantime, he has undergone a subtle transformation. Although he hasn't entirely abandoned his romantic hopes, he has accepted the idea that, if they have a relationship, it is destined to be an open one—a prospect to which he adjusts with very little fuss. The two settle into a remarkably comfortable arrangement, in which they enjoy one another's company, make love with undiminished enthusiasm, and venture out on joint escapades to the baths and backrooms. In the Brian-Justin saga, in other words, the dialectic of love and lust remains richly unresolved. It is the clearest instance of the show's rejection of the binary categories into which conservatives are inclined to press gay relationships.

* * *

The group of friends also includes two lesbians: Melanie, a dark-haired Jewish lawyer, and Lindsay, a blond WASP art teacher. They have been in a relationship for six years. Although both are conventionally attractive, there is more than a hint of the butch-fem opposition, with Melanie wearing the pants in the family. Lindsay is very much the wife: in the opening episode she gives birth to a son. The sperm donor is none other than Brian, who went to college with Lindsay and with whom she was more than a little in love. Much of the intrigue in the story derives from the fact that Melanie quite loathes Brian, while Lindsay retains a lingering affection.

One suspects that the inclusion of this lesbian couple was inspired by a desire to be evenhanded, as well as to promote the ideal of gay and lesbian solidarity. It suggests a connectedness between gay and lesbian lives that, in my experience at least, rarely exists. Admittedly, the gay men and the lesbians are often at odds. The men regularly make nasty remarks about dykes—or "munchers"—while the lesbians for their part are continually appalled by the sexual excesses of the men, especially Brian. But they are nonetheless shown to be genuine friends, elaborately involved in one another's daily experiences.

There is one crucial difference between the men and the women: the women are no longer engaged in the dialectic of lust and love that is the leitmotif in the lives of the men. The show thus supports the widely accepted view that gay men are inclined to be sexual adventurers, while lesbians are nesters. To be sure, Melanie and Lindsay are fully sexual creatures, and their lovemaking is as graphically portrayed as that of the men (causing a certain queasiness among gay male viewers). Nor are they entirely immune to outside temptations. When Lindsay neglects her after the childbirth, Melanie has a brief fling with another woman, which prompts Lindsay to kick her out. Infidelity is a serious offense, much more so than for the men. Later, when they suffer a bout of the dread Lesbian "bed death," they are rescued by a three-way with Melanie's former girlfriend. But they promptly return to their faithful ways. Sexually, gays and lesbians are shown to occupy separate universes. As Melanie puts it, "Women know how to commit to each other. Men don't, at least not the men I know."

Another (related) difference between the men and the women is that Melanie and Lindsay decide to get married. The decision and the complications it gives rise to provide the second season with its dramatic centerpiece. The men, especially Brian, sometimes ridicule them for aping this central convention of straight society, but in the end they all come to the women's support: when various difficulties threaten to delay the wedding, the men pitch in to bring it off on time and in style. Strikingly, there is almost no discussion of the pros and cons of gay marriage, no awareness of the opposing arguments that have set Andrew Sullivan and Michael Warner against one another. Most important, none of the men—not even those in relationships— gives so much as a passing thought to the idea that he too might want to get married. Marriage in the world of *Queer as Folk* is strictly for lesbians—and, of course, for straights. In effect, Andrew Sullivan's proposed solution to the gay predicament is nowhere on the conceptual horizon.

*   *   *

While *Queer as Folk*, like any good soap opera, is mainly concerned with relationships, it does not neglect politics. Homophobia is an ever present threat. Justin must put up with the fag-baiting of his school-mates, while Michael (who's in the closet at work) has to listen to his colleagues' antiqueer jokes. Much more seriously, Justin is severely bashed by a fellow student—to whom he has given a hand job—and must endure a trial in which his assailant gets off with a slap on the wrist. Later, Michael's uncle Vic, who has AIDS, is entrapped in a public urinal, giving rise to another wrenching trial. In the second season one of the boys from Babylon is murdered (as it turns out, by a cop who was paying him for sex). It is the occasion for great outrage and a campaign for justice, which is led by Michael's almost comically homophile mother, Debbie, herself a central character in the show, at once an object of fun for her excesses in the cause and an emotional mainstay for all the friends. Politics comes center stage in the third season, when the main plot line turns on the mayoral candidacy of the homophobic police chief, who has shut down the bathhouses and backrooms and promises to clean up the gay ghetto. The character is clearly modeled on Rudolph Giuliani, another law enforcement figure turned mayor, who tried to dismantle much of New York's gay sexual culture, giving rise, of course, to Michael Warner's Sex Panic. Led again by Debbie, the gay community fights back, and the season ends with dancing in the streets when the chief is defeated.

The idea that gays constitute a community—one that is under siege from hostile forces—is a constant theme of the show. It is suggested, *in nuce*, by the solidarity of the little group of friends. For all their disagreements and sometimes sharp antagonisms, they are firmly attached to one another, and that attachment provides the show with a palpable emotional tug. The most intense moment of solidarity—and the subject of the most moving of the episodes—is Gay Pride day, with its culminating parade. Debbie calls it "the high homo holiday." The episode begins by establishing a number of petty conflicts between the characters. Melanie wants to ride with the Dykes on Bikes, while Lindsay wants them to march with the Marriage Initiative. Justin—for whom this is his "first Pride"—is reluctant to march with his mother, who is a new recruit to PFLAG (Parents and Friends of Lesbians and Gays). Much to Debbie's chagrin, Michael refuses to march because he fears being found out by his homophobic coworkers, who make a habit of attending the parade to mock the freaks. Emmett is in mourning because an old black drag queen, Godiva, who took him under her wing when he first arrived in Pittsburgh, has just died. Only unprepossessing Ted is in a good mood, because he has been the beneficiary of a "pity fuck" by a hunky guy who makes a practice of offering his favors to some sexually needy soul on Gay Pride. In the conventional manner of such narratives, all these difficulties are transcended so that the friends can come together in the more perfect union of the parade. Most spectacularly, Michael marches in Godiva's drag—thereby thrilling his mother—and kisses his faggot-hating boss. The parade itself is perfectly designed to give Bruce Bawer serious indigestion. The street is awash in rainbow bunting, the crowd is festive, and the contingents include not just Dykes on Bikes and lots of near naked men but a healthy supply of drag queens as well. Far from the shameful display of immodesty denounced by Bawer, Gay Pride is an emotionally resonant expression of the community's sense of identity and purpose.

Only Brian does not march. Although he often works in secret to promote the interests of the community, he is deeply cynical about politics and any display of political enthusiasm. In part, this attitude reflects his radical individualism: he is very much the self-made man, a kind of Social Darwinist, who views collective action as a sign of weakness. But, more fundamentally, he considers Gay Pride a confession of gay shame. Only because gays actually take the hostile opinions of straights seriously do they need to puff themselves up with a public assertion of their self-love. In other words, his contempt for straight society is so pure that it can be expressed only through utter indifference. "Who gives a flying fuck what straight people think?" he asks. In his idiosyncratic way Brian is an extraordinarily radical figure, the dramatic counterpart, one might argue, of Michael Warner.

* * *

I suggested above that Babylon represented Pittsburgh's version of the circuit. The circuit proper exists only on the margins of the show. It is first mentioned at a dinner party when Michael accuses one of the guests of having given him crabs at the White Party. It figures much more prominently, and in an ideologically interesting way, in the lesbian wedding episode. Brian wins a trip to the White Party in Miami and invites Justin to come along. But the party conflicts with the date for the wedding. Without much fret, Brian decides in favor of Miami ("I'd rather get laid"), while Justin, after considerable agonizing, forgoes the adventure and attends the ceremony. The show cleverly sets the wedding, with its emotional gravitas, against the image of Brian dancing ecstatically amidst hundreds of buff young men on a collective high. One might say that the episode poses the great gay choice between responsible domesticity ("life outside") and Dionysian bliss ("life inside"). Significantly, the matter is left unresolved, although when Lindsay and Melanie toss their bouquet, it mysteriously lands in Brian's hand on the dance floor 1,200 miles away. In the third season, the circuit appears in a much more menacing guise: some sleazy acquaintances seduce Ted into going to the White Party in Palm Springs, where, drugged into unconsciousness, he is sodomized by one man after another. Here the circuit is seen very much as Michelangelo Signorile portrays it in *Life Outside.*

In a broader sense, many aspects of gay life that Signorile links to the circuit figure prominently in the show. Most obviously, all of the men are obsessed with their bodies and attend the gym religiously. Indeed, scenes set in the gym (and in its erotically charged steam room) are almost as common as scenes in Babylon. There is much talk about abs and pecs, and in one episode Emmett looks into the possibility of butt implants. Similarly, all the men take drugs. Brian in particular is a virtuoso indulger, treating himself to an amazing variety and quantity of illegal substances, along with poppers, alcohol, and cigarettes. At one point Ted tries Viagra and gets an erection that won't go away (which, of course, is played for laughs). In the third season Michael's lover becomes hooked on steroids, which he takes ostensibly for his HIV infection but really to give himself bigger muscles.

For the most part the show refuses to be alarmist about drugs: they are presented as an integral feature of gay life, a source of fun and unobjectionable erotic stimulation. But their dangers are not ignored. Ted's twink boyfriend is seriously addicted to crystal meth and is forced to go into rehabilitation. Ted himself sees his life fall apart as he is sucked into the drug culture of the circuit. Eventually he too is forced into rehabilitation. In a scene that is at once ironic and touching, he is met there by his old boyfriend, who has not only righted himself but become a drug counselor. Drugs, in other words, are seen as a mixed blessing. While viewed much more indulgently than they are by Signorile, they are nonetheless shown to have their perils.

Signorile's main objection to the circuit is that it encourages unsafe sex and thus threatens a revival of the AIDS epidemic. AIDS is also a constant, though not an overwhelming, presence in *Queer as Folk*. We see it mainly in the diminished form it has assumed since protease inhibitors were introduced in the mid-1990s. It is represented most prominently by Michael's uncle Vic, who has been brought back from the edge of death by the new drugs. He is a worn and hollow figure, a shadow of his once glamorous self, tied to a grueling routine of pills and forced to live with his sister. Later in the show the issue assumes more dramatic weight when Michael's lover turns out to be HIV-positive. His mother and friends want Michael to end the relationship, but he overcomes his (and their) fears, and the show is able to explore the delicate emotional and physical negotiations such a relationship entails.

All of the men have adopted the same policy for dealing with the threat of infection: they practice safer sex. In other words, they subscribe wholeheartedly to the condom code that Gabriel Rotello criticizes as inadequate, indeed as dangerous, because it encourages "anal multipartnerism." Debbie hands out condoms to the customers in her diner. Emmett gets tested every six months and calls himself "a poster boy for safe sex." Later, he and Michael are appalled when they find themselves at a barebacking party. The theme of safer sex is introduced brilliantly in the series's opening episode. As Justin is about to lose his virginity, he says hesitatingly to Brian, "At school we have this lecture about safe sex." Handing him a condom, Brian responds, "And now we're going to have a demonstration. Put it on me. Go on, slip it on my dick." The lesson is reinforced when, in the second season, Justin suggests that, unlike Michael and his HIV-positive boyfriend, they can have unprotected intercourse. Brian is uncompromising: "You want me to fuck you bareback? Fuck yourself, you stupid little bastard. Never let anyone fuck you without a condom." It sounds rather brutal, but in fact he says it with affection. After they make love, Brian tells Justin, "I want you safe. I want you around for a long time."

The show refuses to contemplate the possibility, urged by Gabriel Rotello, that the sexual behavior of its characters might be an invitation to "ecological" disaster. I don't of course mean that it actually engages Rotello's argument and rejects it. The issue doesn't exactly lend itself to dramatic representation. But, more fundamentally, the show is unambiguously committed to a celebratory view of gay sexuality. Ideologically it is much closer to sex radicals like Michael Warner and Eric Rofes than to naysayers like Signorile and Rotello.

We are back where we began: *Queer as Folk*'s raison d'être and the source of its claim to cultural significance is its portrayal of gay sex without euphemism and in all its glory. The first line we hear in the first episode, as the camera pans over Babylon, is "The thing you need to know is it's all about sex." AIDS can't be allowed to cast too dark a shadow over this erotic tableau. The threat of disfiguration and death lurks somewhere in the back of everyone's mind, but it occupies much less mental space than the more certain—and perhaps more dreaded—prospect of growing old.

INDEX

ACT UP, 20, 27, 59, 116; and Rotello, 128; and Signorile, 104–5, 117, 118, 128

After the Ball (Kirk and Madsen), 9, 34

AIDS epidemic: in Africa, 130; anal multipartnerism behavior, 129–32, 135–39, 141–42, 145–46, 147–48; circuit parties, 66–67, 110–11, 117, 124, 143; "condom code," 133, 135–36, 141, 161; "core group" concept, 129–30, 131–32, 141–42, 144, 146; drug use, unsafe sex, 111–12; "the fear," 9, 76, 126; friendship culture, 71; intravenous drug users, 130–31; *Longtime Companion* (film), 39; and cult of masculinity, 115; negotiated safety practice, 135, 145; "Patient Zero," 124; political effects of, 6; post-AIDS era, 143; promiscuity, 9, 20, 59, 62; *Queer as Folk* (TV series), 161–62; revival of, 124, 125–26, 127; Rofes's views on, 143–47; sense of responsibility, 75–76; universal gay death fear, 141

alliance politics, 17–18, 79, 85–86

anal multipartnerism behavior, 129–32, 133, 135–39, 141–42, 145–46, 147–48; negotiated safety practice, 135, 145

And the Band Played On: Politics, People, and the AIDS Epidemic (Shilts), 9, 124

public vs. private, 21. *See also* outing
    closeted homosexuals
Coming Out Conservative (Liebman), 4
condom code, 133, 135–36, 141, 161
Connerly, Ward, 4
conservatism: alliance politics, 17–18;
    gay sexual behavior, 2, 4, 9–10, 11;
    gender deviance, 2, 11; hard-headed
    realism, 7; material interests of, 7–8;
    politics, 2. *See also* gay conservatives;
    specific individuals
Construction of Homosexuality, The
    (Greenberg), 56
"core group" concept of AIDS epidemic,
    129–30, 131–32, 141–42, 144, 146
Coulter, Ann, 4
Crimp, Douglas, 68, 70
*The Culture of Desire: Paradox and Perver-
    sity in Gay Lives Today* (Browning),
    30–31

Dancer from the Dance (Holleran), 29
Davis, Bette, 27
Defense of Marriage Act (DOMA), 106
Democratic Party, 1
"deurbanization" of homosexuality,
    119–23
Dinshaw, Carolyn, 134–35
DOMA (Defense of Marriage Act), 106
*Dry Bones Breathe: Gay Men Creating
    Post-AIDS Identities and Cultures*
    (Rofes), 74–76, 143. *See also* Rofes,
    Eric
Duberman, Martin, 139, 147
Dugas, Gaetan, 124

effeminacy, 2, 34; Bawer on, 83, 97; and
    circuit parties, 113; discouragement
    of, 11, 13–14, 25–26; of Gay Pride
    parades, 26–27, 80; in *Queer as Folk*,
    154; Sullivan on, 80, 82–83

"fairy culture," 131
female conservatism, 4
Finnis, John, 50
Forbes, Malcolm, 107
Foucault, Michael, 42, 45; conception
    of homosexuality of, 56, 57; on
    Greek male sexual behavior, 137; and
    outing, 58
Fourier, Charles, 93
Freud, Sigmund, 142; historical pes-
    simism of, 7; homosexuality origins,
    57–58
Fumento, Michael, 39

*Gay and Gray: The Older Homosexual
    Man* (Berger), 122
gay conservatives: about men by
    men, 3; AIDS epidemic effects, 6;
    constructs of homosexuality of,
    22; and Gay Liberation movement,
    1–2, 3, 5, 8; gay marriage, 6;
    gays in the military, 6; gender
    nonconformity, 12–13; generational
    shift, 3; radicalism vs. maturity,
    12; sentimental romanticism, 16;
    terminology, 2; voting economic
    interests, 5. *See also specific individual
    or issue*
Gay Liberation movement, 1, 118;
    and conservatism, 5, 17; gender
    radicalism of, 113; multipartner anal
    sex, 131; Stonewall generation, 3, 5,
    8, 17, 59, 78, 93, 94, 116, 120, 121
gay marriage: Andrew Sullivan on, 60,
    62–64, 69–70, 79; Bruce Bawer on,
    32–33; and decrease of homophobia,
    63; gay children, 62; legal equality,
    61; Michael Warner on, 89–90, 91–
    93political issue of, 6; psychological
    effects of, 63–64; sexual behavior
    changes, 62–63; social approval, 63

Lesbian Avengers, 20

lesbians: marginalization of, 3; promiscuity, 29; serial monogamy, 134–35. *See also* mannish women

The Letters of the Republic: Publication and the Public Sphere in Eighteenth-Century America (Warner), 89

Lewis, Lynette, 144

liberalism, 45, 52–55, 60–64

liberationists, 45, 55–64, 75, 87

Liebman, Marvin, 4

Life Outside (Signorile), 104, 105, 109–10. *See also* Signorile, Michelangelo

Log Cabin Republican Club, 2, 5

Long, Margaret, 134–35

Longtime Companion (film), 39

Love Undetectable: Notes on Friendship, Sex, and Survival (Sullivan), 43, 57, 59, 65, 70, 71, 127

Madsen, Hunter, 9; AIDS epidemic, 10; book tone, 34; counteracting antigay prejudice, 10–15; effeminism, discouragement of, 13–14; gender noncomformity, 12–13; as marketing expert, 10; sexual misbehavior, criticism of, 14–15

The Male Couple: How Relationships Develop (McWhirter and Mattison), 120–21

Mann, William, 122

mannish women, 80; discouragement of, 2, 13–14, 16, 25–26

Mansfield, Harvey, 44

Marcuse, Herbert, 93

marriage. *See* gay marriage

Martin, Ricky, 108

Matalin, Mary, 4

Mattison, Andrew, 120–21

McWhirter, David, 120–21

Melancholia and Moralism: Essays on AIDS and Queer Politics (Crimp), 68

The Men from the Boys (Mann), 122

military. *See* gays in the military

Mill, John Stuart, 52, 60

Minkowitz, Donna, 29

Monette, Paul, 28–29

Nader, Ralph, 3

NAMBLA (North American Man-Boy Love Association), 26

National Gay and Lesbian Task Force, 52, 79, 82, 84

neoconservatives, 103–4

New York Native (magazine), 40–41

Noonan, Peggy, 4

North American Man-Boy Love Association (NAMBLA), 26

Oakeshott, Michael, 44

O'Connor, John (cardinal), 104

Odets, Walt, 139, 145

O'Donnell, Rosie, 108

On Liberty (Mill), 60

oral sex behavior, 136–37

O'Rourke, P. J., 39

outing closeted homosexuals, 58, 104–9

Paglia, Camile, 3

"Patient Zero," 124

Pattullo, E. L., 50–52

pederasty, 137

pedophilia, 26, 89; within Roman Catholic Church, 44, 49

A Place at the Table (Bawer), 10, 16–23, 34, 105, 128. *See also* Bawer, Bruce

procreative sex, 48, 50

prohibitionists, 44, 49

promiscuity, 4, 10, 11, 28–30; AIDS epidemic and, 6, 59, 76–77; Andrew Sullivan on, 59, 62–63, 64–70;

promiscuity (*continued*)
  bathhouse sex, 30, 59, 88, 114, 117, 131, 138, 147; genderbending, 18, 26–27, 80, 96; Michael Warner's view on, 89, 91–93, 141–42; repression's affect on, 65–66, 80; Richard Goldstein on, 96; unprotected sex, 125–28. *See also* unprotected sex

Queer as Folk (cable TV series): age-consciousness in, 153; AIDS in, 161–62; Brian (character), 154–56, 161–62; circuit issues, 159–60; community of gays depicted in, 158–59; and contemporary gay reality, 152, 162; drug culture, 160–61; Emmett (character), 154; gay and lesbian solidarity in, 156–57; gay marriage in, 157, 159–60; Gay Pride episode, 158–59; gym scenes, 160; homophobia in, 157–58; Lindsay (character), 156, 159–60; lust and love, 152–53, 155–56, 159–60; Melanie (character), 156, 159–60; Michael (character), 153–54; political themes, 157–59; popularity, impact of, 151–52; safer sex theme, 161–62; sex club scenes in, 152–53, 155; Ted (character), 153
Queer in America (Rotello), 105. *See also* Rotello, Gabriel
Queer Nation, 20, 116
queer versus gay label, 58–59, 105

racism, 17–18, 26, 45, 85, 86–87; antidiscrimination legislation versus individual liberty, 53; constructs of, 54
Raines, Howell, 100
Ratzinger, Joseph (cardinal), 46, 49, 104

Reno, Janet, 108
Reviving the Tribe: Regenerating Gay Men's Sexuality and Culture in an Ongoing Epidemic (Rofes), 143. *See also* Rofes, Eric
Rofes, Eric, 74–75, 149; circuit behavior, 144–45; on Gabriel Rotello, 143, 144, 145–46; on Michelangelo Signorile, 144–45; negotiated safety, 145; sexual liberation, 143–47
Roman Catholicism: exclusion of women from the priesthood in, 82; homophobia, 71; on homosexuality, 48, 49; homosexual priests, 101
Ross, Michael, 144
Rotello, Gabriel, 2, 93; ACT UP, 128; AIDS epidemic, 129; anal multipartnerism behavior, 129–32, 133, 135–39, 141–42, 145–46, 147–48; circuit parties, 117, 143; "condom code," 133, 135–36, 141, 161; "core group" concept of AIDS epidemic, 129–30, 131–32, 141–42, 144, 146; and Eric Rofes, 143, 144, 145–46; "fairy culture," 131; lesbian serial monogamy, 134–35; and Michelangelo Signorile, 128–29; monogamy, 134–39; negotiated safety practice, 135; as neoconservative, 103–4; outing closeted homosexuals, 104–5; sexual behavior, 4, 124, 162; sexual conservatism of, 147–49; sexual moralism of, 139–42, 148; universal gay death fear of, 141, 142; unprotected sex increase, 112, 117, 141, 162
Ryan, Alan, 61

Sacred Band of Thebes legend, 81
Same-Sex Marriage: Pro and Con (Sullivan), 62
Santorum, Rick, 101